TOMBSTONE

Wyatt Earp, The O.K. Corral, and the Vendetta Ride 1881–82

SEAN McLACHLAN

First published in Great Britain in 2013 by Osprey Publishing,
Midland House, West Way, Botley, Oxford, OX2 0PH, UK
43-01 21st Street, Suite 220B, Long Island City, NY 11101
E-mail: info@ospreypublishing.com

Osprey Publishing is part of the Osprey Group

A CIP catalog record for this book is available from the British Library

Print ISBN: 978 1 78096 192 7
PDF ebook ISBN: 978 1 78096 193 4
ePub ebook ISBN: 978 1 78096 194 1

Index by Marie-Pierre Evans
Typeset in Sabon
Maps by bounford.com
Originated by PDQ Media, Bungay, UK
Printed in China through Worldprint Ltd

13 14 15 16 17 10 9 8 7 6 5 4 3 2 1

DEDICATION

To my wife, Almudena, and my son, Julián.

ACKNOWLEDGMENTS

Numerous researchers helped with the preparation of this book. I would like to thank the staff at the Arizona Historical Society and the Arizona State Library Archives for help in digging up photos, and author David Lee Summers for some up-to-date images and insights into Tombstone. All photos credited (LoC) are courtesy of the Library of Congress, Prints and Photographs Division.

AUTHOR'S NOTE

As anyone working in law enforcement will attest, most people make terrible witnesses. The events in Tombstone were recorded in numerous letters, diaries, newspaper reports, and official documents. It seems that everyone who was there – and many who weren't – wanted to tell their part in the drama and support their personal opinion. Then as now, newspaper reporters were not averse to making things up in order to add zest to a story or to fill in the blanks. Thus the accounts of the events in and around Tombstone are often contradictory. Also, the history of Tombstone has been plagued by careless or biased writers who muddled facts or made up events. In this book we have chosen the majority opinions and assembled a consistent narrative from them. Important variants are also mentioned. Those interested in the many other twists to this tale are referred to the Bibliography.

ARTIST'S NOTE

Readers may care to note that the original paintings from which the color plates on pages 28–29 and 70–71 of this book were prepared are available for private sale. All reproduction copyright whatsoever is retained by the Publishers. All inquiries should be addressed to:

mark@mrstacey.plus.com

The Publishers regret that they can enter into no correspondence upon this matter.

EDITOR'S NOTE

For ease of comparison please refer to the following conversion table:

1 mile = 1.6km
1yd = 0.9m
1ft = 0.3m
1in. = 2.54cm/25.4mm
1 gallon (U.S.) = 3.8 liters
1 ton (U.S.) = 0.9 metric tons
1lb = 0.45kg

CONTENTS

INTRODUCTION

Wyatt Earp is one of the legends of the Wild West. He has been portrayed numerous times in film and countless times in fiction as everything from a squeaky-clean crime fighter to a corrupt gunslinger. As with all Wild West legends, the truth is more complex and far more interesting than the fiction.

His father, Nicholas Porter Earp, was a veteran of the war with Mexico whose brief term of service ended when he got kicked in the groin by a mule. This didn't prevent his wife getting pregnant, however, and Wyatt Berry Stapp Earp was born on March 19, 1848. Wyatt was Nicholas' fourth son, after Newton, James (Jim), and Virgil. Two more, Morgan and Warren, were to follow. The family lived in various places, including Kentucky, Illinois, and Iowa.

When the Civil War broke out in 1861, Newton, James, and Virgil went off to fight for the Union. James came home with a shoulder wound that crippled one of his arms. To get away from the war, Nicholas took his family to California in 1864. The 16-year-old Wyatt distinguished himself by hunting for meat along the way and helping fight off two Indian raids against the wagon train.

Wyatt didn't have the temperament to be a farmer's son, and soon he and Virgil went to seek their fortune. In 1870, Wyatt got a job as constable in Lamar, Missouri, where he handled the town's small population of drunks and criminals with efficiency and diplomacy. When he left near the end of the year, however, he was accused of embezzling $20 of town funds. For some reason the charges were dropped. Wyatt, now 22, moved to the Indian Territory, modern Oklahoma, where he was charged with stealing two horses. Once again the details are unclear, and once again he was never brought to trial. Some biographers believe he actually jumped bail. His supposed accomplice was acquitted. These two incidents placed a stain on Wyatt's early days that has kept researchers arguing ever since.

Wyatt continued wandering, working various jobs on the Frontier such as hunting buffalo. He ended up in the cow town of Ellsworth, Kansas, where he became marshal after the previous one was shot dead. Although in modern American slang the term "cow town" is reserved for boring hick villages, the original cow towns were anything but. These were the days of the great range drives, when vast herds of cattle were moved up from Texas to the meatpacking plants of Kansas City. The railroad then shipped the meat all over the country. The cattlemen made regular stops on the long ride north and towns grew rich fleecing the men with expensive booze, crooked card games, and loose women. Needless to say, cheating large numbers of drunken Texans led to some rough incidents. Brawls were a daily occurrence and shootings frequent.

Cow towns boomed and busted as routes changed and the railway lines spread across the land. Ellsworth soon faded and Wyatt moved to the now-booming Wichita, which the *St. Louis Republican* described as resembling:

> ... a brevet hell after sundown. Brass bands whooping it up, harlots and hack drivers yelling and cursing; dogs yelping, pistols going off; bull-whackers cracking their whips; saloons open wide their doors, and gaily attired females thump and drum up pianos, and in dulcet tones and mocking smiles invite the boys in and the night is commenced in earnest.

In 1874, 26-year-old Wyatt Earp and his older brother Jim arrived at this "brevet hell." Jim worked as a bartender and his wife Bessie as a prostitute. At that place and time, shacking up with a prostitute wasn't considered scandalous. Women were too scarce on the Frontier to be picky. Wyatt became deputy marshal and also worked as a gambler, also something that was not considered unusual or even disreputable in those days. The dusty towns that popped up on the Frontier were free zones when it came to lifestyles. In Tombstone, Arizona, there was even an openly lesbian couple. Such a thing would have been impossible back East. On the Frontier it elicited only the occasional frown.

The law had to walk a careful line in cow towns. The local economy relied on vice, yet at the same time

Wyatt Earp seated next to Bat Masterson, standing. This photograph was taken in 1876 or 1877 in Dodge City, Kansas, while Wyatt was assistant marshal and Bat was sheriff of Ford County. Wyatt would have been 28 or 29 in this shot and Bat would have been 23 or 24. (Arizona Historical Society, photo #76636)

nobody wanted violence. In cases of anything less than murder, the head drover was usually allowed to buy his boys out of jail. This kept the cattlemen happy and the money flowing in. Wyatt showed himself capable of performing this gentle balancing act on more than one occasion and earned a reputation for toughness, fairness, and an ability to defuse tense situations without resorting to gunplay. When he did use his pistols, it was usually to club some miscreant over the head rather than fill him with lead. Wyatt also had a reputation for honesty. A local paper praised him when he found a drunk passed out in the street with $500 in his pocket. Wyatt put the fellow in the drunk tank with his money intact.

This promising career came to an end when Wyatt got into an election-year fight with his boss's rival for the position of marshal. Once again details are unclear; the newspapers reported that he was fired after being arrested for disturbing the peace. Again at liberty, he got a job as assistant marshal in Dodge City, Kansas. It was during this period of his life that Wyatt met another man destined to become a Western legend – a tubercular dentist named Doc Holliday.

John Henry Holliday was born in 1851 in Georgia to a family of aristocrats and slave owners. He was born with a cleft lip and partially cleft palate. This birth defect made it impossible to breastfeed him and he had to drink his mother's milk from a shot glass. Once he was old enough to undergo surgery the birth defect was fixed, but he was left with a slight speech impediment that made him a shy and withdrawn child. The family slave, Sophie, kept him company by teaching him cards, including old slave

A group of cowboys taking a break at their chuck wagon. These wagons carried the cowboys' food, cooking supplies, and personal effects while they were on the range. Since cowboys had to ride long distances herding and rounding up cattle, they kept a minimum of equipment on their horses. For work and travel over shorter distances, riders rarely brought a wagon along because they could rely on hospitality at local ranches and farms. On the Vendetta Ride, Wyatt Earp and his followers brought along a wagon in order to minimize their contact with local ranchers, some of whom supported the Clanton/McLaury faction. (LoC)

This engraving from an 1867 issue of the popular *Frank Leslie's Illustrated Newspaper* shows Texas cattlemen branding steers on the Texas prairie. America's love affair with the West started early, thanks to illustrated papers and dime novels. (LoC)

gambling games such as "skinning," the predecessor to faro, which would become Holliday's favorite game and main source of income as an adult.

Holliday graduated from Pennsylvania College of Dental Surgery in 1872. The next year he was diagnosed with tuberculosis and headed West, hoping the drier climate would help his lungs. It was there that he fell in with the saloon crowd, spending long nights drinking in smoke-filled rooms. Such a lifestyle was most certainly not what the doctor ordered. It was a rough crowd and Holliday got a reputation for toughness, although the stories of his leaving a trail of bullet-riddled bodies are exaggerated.

When he arrived in Dodge City in June of 1878, Holliday rented an office and placed an ad in the local paper offering his services. Arriving with him was Big-Nose Kate (also known as Big-Nosed Kate), a Hungarian immigrant who worked as a prostitute before meeting Holliday. She was as foul-tempered and fond of the bottle as the gunslinging dentist, and that combination had a serious effect on events that would follow in Tombstone. Another associate of Holliday's, Quebec-born gunfighter and Dodge City lawman Bat Masterson, said of him,

> Holliday had a mean disposition and an ungovernable temper, and under the influence of liquor was a most dangerous man. Physically, Doc Holliday was a weakling who could not have whipped a healthy fifteen-year-old boy in a go-as-you-please fist fight,

A prospector's monument in Cochise County, Arizona. Prospectors marked their claim with the claim deed stuck inside a tin can buried under a pile of rocks. The tradition dates back to the earliest prospecting period and continued well into the 20th century. This photo was taken in 1940. Prospectors still wander the Southwest, searching for their version of the American Dream. (LoC)

NOVEMBER 27, 1879

Virgil Earp appointed deputy U.S. marshal for the southeastern portion of the Arizona Territory

and no one knew this better than himself, and the knowledge of this fact was perhaps why he was so ready to resort to a weapon of some kind whenever he got himself into difficulty. He was hot-headed and impetuous and very much given to both drinking and quarreling, and, among men who did not fear him, was very much disliked … Holliday seemed to be absolutely unable to keep out of trouble for any great length of time. He would no sooner be out of one scrape before he was in another, and the strange part of it is he was more often in the right than in the wrong, which has rarely ever been the case with a man who is continually getting himself into trouble.

It should surprise no one to learn that Wyatt and Holliday first became friends because of a gunfight. Two Texas drovers started causing trouble in a saloon and Wyatt and another officer went in to stop them. The lawmen tried to subdue the besotted Texans by pistol-whipping them ("buffaloing" as it was called in those days) but either the liquor or just plain bad attitude kept the drovers on their feet. One pulled a gun and aimed it at Wyatt's back. Holliday, who was playing cards nearby, shouted, "Look out, Wyatt!" and shot at the Texan. Holliday apparently missed, but the gunshot took the fight out of the Texans. It also made Wyatt and Holliday friends for life.

For the most part Wyatt's arrests were not so dramatic, and this is precisely what the citizenry liked about him. The *Dodge City Times* reported that:

> He has a quiet way of taking the most desperate characters into custody which invariably gives one the impression that the city was able to enforce her mandates and preserve her dignity. It wasn't considered policy to draw a gun on Wyatt unless you got the drop and meant to burn powder without any preliminary talk.

DECEMBER 1879

Wyatt, Virgil, and Jim Earp arrive in Tombstone with their wives

At 6ft tall, 180lb, and with an athletic build, Wyatt towered over most men. He had a steely disposition and an understated yet forceful presence. Most troublemakers backed down rather than face him. In fact, there is only one story of Wyatt shooting someone in Dodge. It was that same summer of 1878. A square dance was going on in the Commy-Kew saloon during the small hours of the morning. A banjo player performed on stage to a packed hall while in one corner Bat Masterson dealt a game of Spanish monte with Doc Holliday and some other players. One of the Texans in the crowd had had some sort of quarrel with Wyatt Earp earlier in the evening. Probably the drover had been too rowdy and Wyatt had told him to settle down. Whatever the cause, the drover left in a huff, gathered some friends, and rode past the Commy-Kew. They peppered the front with their six-shooters, the heavy .45 bullets tearing right through the cheap plank boarding. Everyone hit the deck as bullets flew everywhere. Remarkably, no one was hurt.

Wyatt Earp and Jim Masterson, Bat's brother, ran out into the street and ordered the Texans to halt, only to get shot at. Several irate townsmen joined the lawmen and together they returned fire. The Texans fled as one of their number fell off his horse, shot through the arm. Gangrene set in and after being laid up for a month the man died. It is unclear if Wyatt was the one who hit him, but the shootout got the attention of the popular publication *National Police Gazette*. It was Wyatt's first brush with fame.

Cow towns busted as fast as they boomed, and Dodge City was no exception. By 1879, much of the trade was passing it by due to a local drought. Farmers began to stake claims on the surrounding land. This guaranteed it would never be used for cattle grazing again. Wyatt must have seen that Dodge City was dying and wondered where the next opportunity lay. Then came a letter from Virgil. He had settled in Arizona and told Wyatt of the fabulous wealth coming out of the silver mines there. Wyatt decided to head to the Southwest in search of fortune.

ORIGINS

Tombstone got its start in 1877 when prospector Ed Schieffelin filed two mining claims in the San Pedro Valley in the southern Arizona hills. He had been told by local soldiers at Fort Huachuca that the place was crawling with Apaches, scorpions, and rattlesnakes and that he'd only find his tombstone there, so he named his claims Graveyard and Tombstone. Schieffelin struck a rich vein of silver. Soon a steady trickle of miners arrived to stake their own claims. As the trickle turned into a flood, saloons, shops, and boarding houses sprang up. The American West had another boomtown. By 1879 the town had a population of 900 and even had a newspaper, the *Nugget*. The next year former Indian agent John Clum opened the *Epitaph* and soon the two papers were on opposite sides of pretty much every political issue.

The town was well situated on Goose Flats, an open upland with an elevation of 4,500ft that cut down on the heat somewhat. There was a pleasant vista of hills and mountains all around, the biggest being the rugged Dragoon Mountains eight miles to the east, where Apaches still prowled.

Wyatt arrived with his wife Celia Ann "Mattie" Blaylock (she used "Earp" as a last name while she was with Wyatt) in December of 1879, along with brothers Virgil and Jim and their families. All three brothers seem to have had common-law marriages; no marriage certificates have ever been discovered. Virgil had been appointed U.S. deputy marshal, his responsibilities including investigating federal offenses and helping local law enforcement with local problems. Wyatt rode shotgun on Wells Fargo stagecoaches, guarding miners' bankrolls and money transfers. Morgan arrived in July of 1880 and also found work as a shotgun messenger and was at times a special deputy. One-armed Jim tended bar. Warren drifted in and out of Tombstone.

While Wyatt earned a regular income at Wells Fargo, he was also a prominent gambler. His favorite game was faro, and like Doc Holliday he played it with great skill. All of the Earp brothers got together to stake mining claims, which they saw as the real path to riches in this dusty town.

Wyatt and his brothers made tidy profits by staking claims and reselling them to investors. Mining was Wyatt's true passion and the one profession he never entirely gave up.

Tombstone has entered American mythology as the stereotypical shoot-'em-up Western town. This was only half the truth. It was a functioning community with all the regular institutions, one where people worked hard. The reality of Tombstone for most people was a dreary ten-hour day, six-day week working the mines. They lived in wretched shacks as dirty as the mines they worked. A miner's most prized possession wasn't a gun but a cat. Cats were essential to good sleep, as they ate the rats that would crawl over the miners at night and disturb their slumber. A miner had to guard his cat, as cat theft was one of the most common crimes.

Photograph/postcard of Ed Schieffelin, founder of Tombstone. The postcard was a promotional piece for the C.S. Fly Studios (a.k.a. Fly's Photo Gallery) in Tombstone. (Arizona State Library, Archives and Public Records: History and Archives Division)

Although the saloons, whorehouses, and gambling halls get the most attention, Tombstone also had a thriving retail district that grew in size and quality with every year. There was even an ice-cream stand that was a favorite of Wyatt Earp's. Churches started almost immediately after the town's founding, usually in structures almost as flimsy as the miners' shacks. In 1880, diarist George Parsons wrote about attending one service and hardly being able to hear the preacher because of the noise coming from the dance hall next door. Parsons had left a respectable job as a bank clerk in San Francisco to seek his fortune in the mines. His new home put his conservative sensibilities sorely to the test. He noted in his journal, "One must rely entirely upon himself and trust *no one* else." His diary is the most complete account of life in Tombstone at that time, and is also an account of how a straitlaced clerk became a rough Indian hunter and loyal partisan of the Earps.

The ladies of the evening who worked next to the church often attended services. On the Frontier, the strict divisions between respectability and sin were blurred. Perhaps the menfolk were a little more accepting because of the severe shortage of other women in the town's early days. With few

Tombstone in 1881, when the mining town was at the height of its boom period. It would continue to expand for a few years before the mines started to play out in the late 1880s and the town slipped into decline.

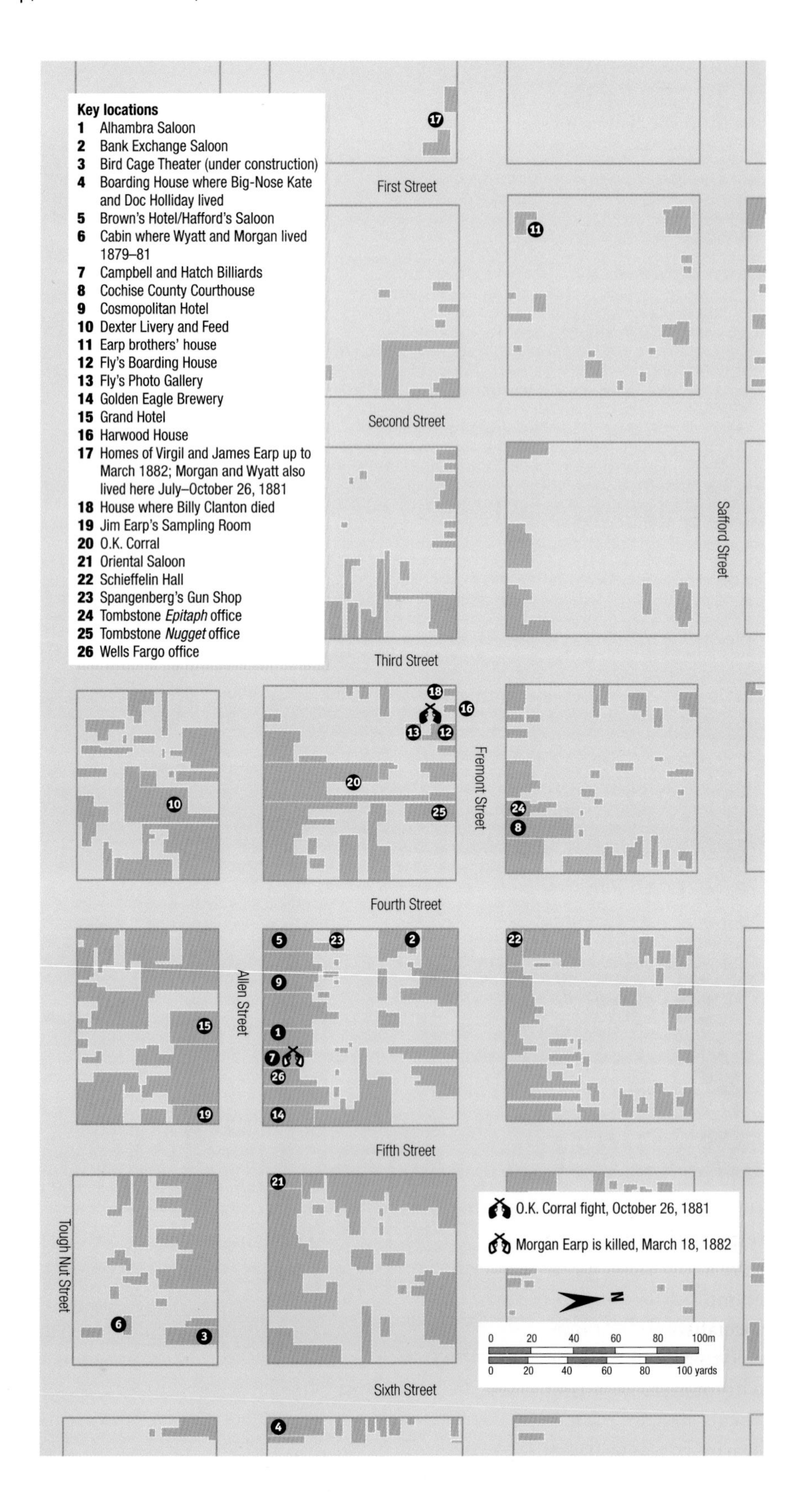

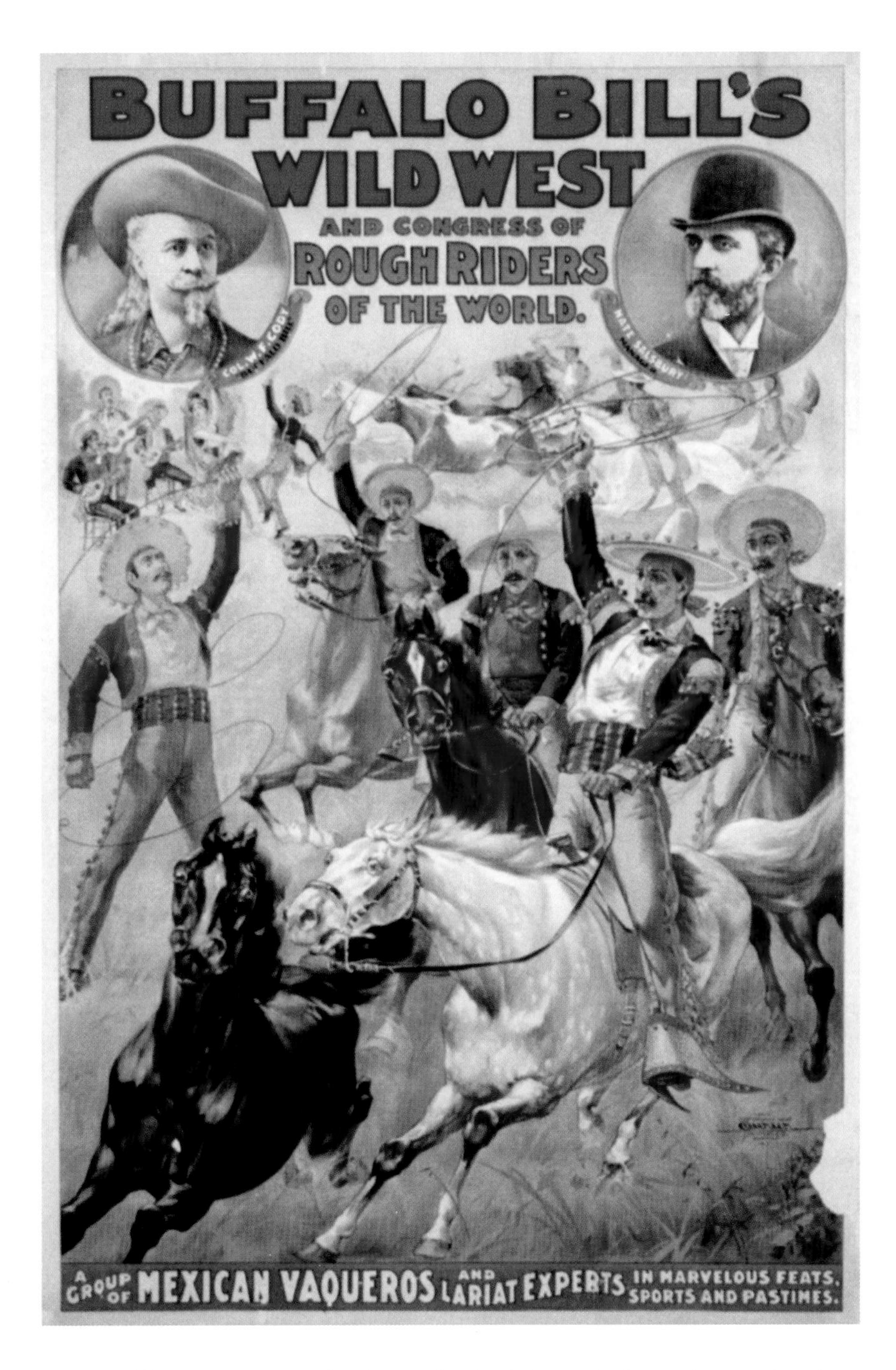

The first cowboys in the Southwest were, of course, the Spanish and later Mexican *vaqueros*. While this has been forgotten in modern times, back in 1899 they were a star attraction in Buffalo Bill's Wild West Show, where their tricks with the lariat amazed audiences. The rope tricks had practical applications on the range, but the flashy costumes would have been left in the bunkhouse. (LoC)

respectable women around, miners plunked down their hard-earned cash to have a drink or a dance with girls such as Crazy Horse Lil, Lizette the Flying Nymph or, if they were really desperate, Madam Moustache. There were specialists too, as one business card attests: "Elderly gentlemen would do well to ask for Maxine in the upper parlor. She is especially adept at coping with matters peculiar to advanced age and a general run-down condition." Locals had to compete for the ladies' attentions with the soldiers from nearby Fort Huachuca, who came into town every payday to whoop it up.

Life on the Frontier forts was hard. Even the commanding officers, such as this one c. 1870 at Camp Colorado in the Arizona Territory, lived rough with their families. It was no wonder, then, that soldiers coming into towns like Tombstone went out on sprees. (LoC)

Civilization was beginning to get a foothold despite all this carousing. The first school opened in 1880, a slapdash affair with a flour barrel for a teacher's desk and seats made of planks set on kegs. By the end of that year Tombstone had an estimated population of up to 7,000. New theaters appeared and competed with the saloons and dance halls for the miners' money. As was usual with these Frontier boomtowns, most people who got rich did so not by mining but by "mining the miners." Ed Schieffelin himself got into the act by building Schieffelin Hall, at 130ft long the largest adobe structure in the country at that time. It was two storeys high, could seat 700, and doubled as the Masonic Hall. Class acts from California performed there. The Bird Cage was another popular theater, with less classy acts and a more riotous audience. Today tourists can still see bullet holes in its ceiling. Thus entertainment befitting both the higher and lower brows could be had in Tombstone. As Parsons noted in his diary one day, "Hanging in the A.M. and Dance in the P.M. Good combination."

Tombstone in the early days is richly described by Clara Spalding Brown. Her husband was a mining engineer and she wrote for the *San Diego Union*. Big-city papers often covered the boomtowns, which were the dreams of many Americans who never so much as visited one. In one article Brown wrote:

> We beheld an embryo city of canvas, frame and adobe, scattered over a slope ... It is a place more pretentious than I had imagined, and full of activity, notwithstanding the hundreds of loungers on the streets. The only attractive places visible are the liquor and

gambling saloons, which are everywhere present and are carpeted and comfortably furnished ... The camp is one of the dirtiest places in the world ... and one is never sure of having a clean face, despite repeated ablutions. It is time to talk about dirt. The sod lies loose upon the surface, and is whirled into the air every day by a wind which almost amounts to a gale; it makes the eyes smart like the cinders from an engine; it penetrates into the houses, and covers everything with dust ... The mercury gallivants around in the nineties, with altogether too high-minded ideas ... we cannot obtain desirable food for hot weather; fresh vegetables are scarce, and the few fruits in the markets require a very large purse ... The camp is considered a remarkably quiet one – only one murder since my arrival.

Tombstone may have had a low murder rate at this time, but fights were common and Apaches still roamed the hills, stealing livestock and occasionally attacking lone travelers. Tombstone had several Indian scares and on more than one occasion sent bands of armed men out to head off a feared attack. Diarist George Parsons went along for the fun.

The settlers had more to worry about than Apaches. Out in the desert lurked bandits who made their living rustling cattle in Mexico and selling them in Arizona. Sometimes they even plucked cattle from American herds. They soon earned the title "cowboy." In most of the West, "cowboy" simply meant a Texan who handled cattle. Now in southern Arizona the name took on a pejorative meaning, distinct from the respectable "rangeman," "drover," or "cattleman."

Frontier conditions gradually improved for the soldiers. These soldiers in 1886 at Fort Verde, Arizona, enjoyed much better conditions than even a commanding officer 15 years earlier. (LoC)

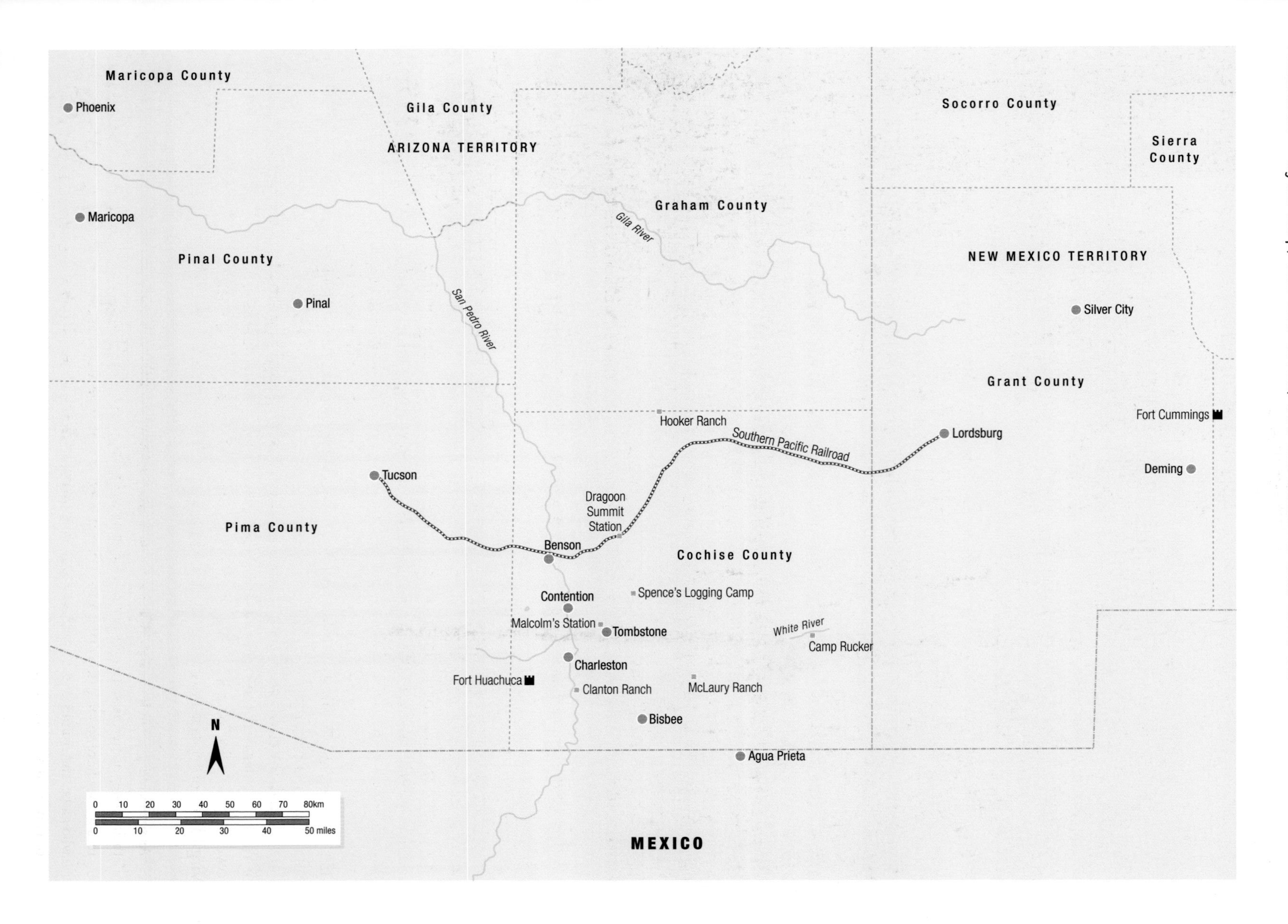
Maricopa County
Phoenix
Gila County
ARIZONA TERRITORY
Socorro County
Sierra County
Maricopa
Graham County
Gila River
Pinal County
NEW MEXICO TERRITORY
Pinal
San Pedro River
Silver City
Grant County
Fort Cummings
Hooker Ranch
Lordsburg
Southern Pacific Railroad
Tucson
Deming
Dragoon Summit Station
Pima County
Benson
Cochise County
Contention
Spence's Logging Camp
Malcolm's Station
Tombstone
White River
Camp Rucker
Charleston
Fort Huachuca
Clanton Ranch
McLaury Ranch
Bisbee
N
Agua Prieta
0 10 20 30 40 50 60 70 80km
0 10 20 30 40 50 miles
MEXICO

Life on the Frontier wasn't all hard work and barroom brawls. The Dodge City Cowboy Band posed for this photo *c.* 1885. Cowboy bands were popular throughout the West, Tombstone included. (LoC)

The cowboys engaged in worse crimes too. They were probably responsible for the area's first attempted stagecoach robbery in May of 1880, in which two gunmen fired upon a coach. The driver kept his head and managed to avoid the robbers, but not before he was shot in the leg and one of his passengers got killed.

Nobody knows how many cowboys there were. The number probably changed wildly over time. Some estimates run up to a couple of hundred, although they were never a rigid organization, more of a loose-knit group of associates who shared the same lifestyle. They stayed on ranches and in small towns, only coming into Tombstone to whoop it up in the closest thing approaching a big city.

Although the cowboys were hardly model citizens, many people supported or at least tolerated them. Their stolen cattle were sold at cut-rate prices, lowering the price of beef. Also, the cowboys had lots of money to spend. Virgil Earp noted with disgust:

> As soon as they are in funds they ride into town, drink, gamble, and fight. They spend their money as free as water in saloons, dancehouses, or faro banks, and this is one reason they have so many friends in town. All that large class of degraded characters who gather the crumbs of such carouses stand ready to assist them out of any trouble or into any paying rascality.

Opposite:
Arizona and New Mexico in 1881–82.

Western Union Telegraph Office and Wells Fargo Express Office in Yuma, Arizona, 1878. These two companies were lifelines for many scattered communities on the Frontier, providing communication and economic links with the outside world. (Arizona State Library, Archives and Public Records: History and Archives Division)

While the cowboys had no real organization, many congregated around two influential ranching families: the Clantons and the McLaurys. Both had large spreads near Tombstone and sizeable herds. Many of the animals were actually stolen south of the border and sold cheap to these two ranching families. Being respected locals, it was easy for them to turn the cattle around and sell them in Tombstone at a good profit. A close look might have revealed that they had been rebranded, and rumors of stolen cattle brought up from the South were rife, but nobody much cared. There were still hard feelings from the Texan War of Independence and the Mexican War.

In July of 1880, Wyatt was appointed deputy sheriff for Tombstone and the surrounding area. Wyatt worked under city marshal Fred White and with fellow deputy sheriff Newton Babcock. It was a tough job. The low murder rate that Mrs Brown had mentioned was going up. An entry in Parsons' diary for April of 1880 reads: "Several more shooting scrapes – but they are of such frequent occurrence that their novelty has ceased." Drunken brawls were a nightly affair. Wyatt also had to deal with horse thieves and other criminals. He had a lot more than a few cattle rustlers to worry about.

As with his previous law-enforcement jobs, Wyatt proved highly capable. Local lawyer William Hunsaker wrote of Wyatt:

> His conduct as a peace officer was above reproach. He was quiet, but absolutely fearless in the discharge of his duties. He usually went about in his shirtsleeves without

> a coat and with no weapon in sight. He was cool and never excited, but determined and courageous. He never stirred up trouble, but he never ran away from it or shirked responsibility. He was an ideal peace officer and a law-abiding citizen.

Things might have gone on fine for the cowboys if they hadn't gotten too rowdy and greedy for their own good. They began to whoop it up in the small communities around Tombstone, shooting into houses and bullying passersby. Resentment grew, and then the cowboys seriously blundered. In July of 1880, some cowboys stole half a dozen U.S. Army mules from Camp Rucker, on the White River 75 miles east of Tombstone. Wyatt, Morgan, and Virgil Earp, plus Wells Fargo agent Marshall Williams, went to find them. Along with some soldiers, they headed out to the McLaury ranch. They had received a tip that the McLaurys, Billy Clanton, and notorious cowboy Charles "Pony" Diehl (sometimes spelled "Deal") were behind the thefts.

They arrived to find them rebranding the mules. A showdown looked likely but the posse, despite having the weight of the law and the U.S. Army on its side, grew nervous. The men were outgunned and on enemy territory. They finally struck a deal that if the mules were returned the next day, no charges would be brought. The mules were never returned and a war of words began between the local Army lieutenant and Frank McLaury, with both taking out newspaper notices to lambast the other. For good measure, McLaury warned Virgil Earp to mind his own business, or else. Virgil reminded him that keeping the law was very much his business and he'd arrest him if given a warrant. The Earp brothers were now marked men.

Cowboys branding cattle in Dakota Territory, *c.* 1888. Each rancher had his own distinct brand registered with the government. Rustlers became skilled at changing brands and often registered a brand that appeared similar to that of their favorite victim. (LoC)

Mrs Ah-Lum, also known as "China Mary," was one of several hundred Chinese who lived in Tombstone during its heyday. She was one of the Chinese community's leading figures, acting as a judge and moneylender. The white community knew her as the head of an employment agency that supplied honest Chinese labor, satisfaction guaranteed. She also owned a large general store stocked with Chinese and American products, and perhaps the only gambling hall in town where Chinese and whites mingled. (LoC)

It seems remarkable to the modern reader that rustlers could steal U.S. Army property and get away with it. In the days before modern criminal investigation methods, however, proof was hard to come by and Frontier courts were notably biased. Also, the rustlers were a power in the land. Perhaps the lieutenant feared he might be the victim of a nighttime shooting. They were not his mules, after all, so perhaps it would be best to let the whole matter drop. With Apaches, smugglers, and fugitives from the law to deal with, the Army must have decided to write off its losses and focus on more important work.

Doc Holliday arrived in Tombstone in September of 1880 and got into his first gunfight there a month later. His target survived with only a shot through the hand. Holliday was hauled before Judge Reilly, who didn't like Wyatt Earp because Earp hadn't taken his side in a petty political fight. The judge found Earp's friend guilty. The witnesses for the prosecution failed to show up, however, and so the judge could only charge the dentist with assault and battery, giving him a fine.

A more serious shooting came that same month. Curley Bill Brocious and some of his fellow cowboys boozed it up on the night of October 28. Curley Bill was prominent among the rustlers, a 6ft-tall handsome charmer who had thick curly black hair that gave him his nickname. Many reports say he was honest with his friends and generally an affable fellow, but when he drank he turned into a ruthless gunman and bully.

Fueled by whiskey, Curley Bill and his crew staggered out into the street and began to shoot at the moon and stars. City marshal Fred White went to disarm them and chased Curley Bill into a vacant lot. Wyatt Earp was not far behind. White caught up with Curley Bill and demanded his gun, at which point the cowboy drew it. Gamely, the marshal grabbed the barrel and yanked. It went off, the bullet hitting the marshal in the groin. Wyatt buffaloed Curley Bill as others carried the grievously wounded marshal away. Fearing his charge might be lynched, Wyatt took Curley Bill up to Tucson and put him in the jail there to await trial. White died two days later.

Tombstone Sheriff John Behan, probably taken at C.S. Fly Studios (a.k.a. Fly's Photo Gallery) *c.* 1885 when he was in his early forties. The dapper Behan charmed Tombstone when he first arrived, but many residents soon soured in their response to him over his ties to the cowboys. (Arizona State Library, Archives and Public Records: History and Archives Division)

There was an outpouring of public grief for the popular marshal and the town council quickly passed an ordinance banning the carrying of guns within city limits. The council appointed Virgil Earp as temporary city marshal but Ben Sippy won the election when it was held shortly thereafter. For Virgil, this was a major economic opportunity lost. Not only did the city marshal's position pay $100 a month, it also received a percentage of city taxes. For a boomtown like Tombstone, that added up to a significant haul.

OCTOBER 28, 1880

Curley Bill Brocious shoots and kills city marshal Fred White

Elections in the decades right after the Civil War highlighted enduring national divisions, and Tombstone was no exception. Most businessmen and other townsfolk were Republican, being of Northern birth or persuasion. The Republicans read the *Epitaph* to find stories and editorials supporting their views. On the other hand, most ranchers, rangemen, and cowboys came from the South, especially Texas, and supported the Democratic Party. They went to the *Nugget* for sympathetic reading. The Republicans wanted a quiet town in order to attract investment, while the Democrats generally winked at the exploits of the cowboys and enjoyed the cheap meat and Mexican gold and silver that the rustlers brought into the region.

This election year also saw a contest between incumbent Pima County sheriff Charlie Shibell, a Democrat, and his Republican opponent Bob Paul. Shibell barely won and many said the election was rife with fraud. Johnny Ringo served as one of the precinct judges and Ike Clanton appears to have served as a voting inspector – both men were cowboys. Curley Bill went around San Simon Valley rounding up men, women, and children to vote for Shibell. Early pioneer James Hancock later recalled that the cowboys "voted all their horses and a dog or two and a stray cat, and finally to make sure no one had been neglected and not been given a chance to cast his ballot, they voted everyone again."

While this seems a case of an old-timer spinning a tale, the *Epitaph* did report that the San Simon tally was 103 to 1. The newspaper added that the lone vote for Paul was cast by a Texas cowboy who wanted to prove that the voting had been honest.

Wyatt Earp didn't approve of such shenanigans and resigned as deputy in order to help with Paul's appeal. The case went through the courts and after much legal wrangling Paul was declared the winner on April 12, 1881. Stepping into Wyatt's shoes as deputy came Johnny Behan, a former territorial representative and sheriff of Yavapai County who had come to Tombstone seeking political advancement. He was popular thanks to his good looks and hail-fellow-well-met style. At first he tried to befriend the Earps, but that friendship was not to last.

The stagecoach routes provided a lifeline for small towns before the arrival of the railroad. This stagecoach, photographed in the late 19th century in Dodge City, Kansas, ran a route from western Kansas to the Oklahoma Territory. (LoC)

Although Wyatt lost the income of his law-enforcement job, he made good money as a faro dealer and enforcer at the Oriental Saloon, the most luxurious drinking and gambling establishment in town and one in which he had purchased a quarter partnership in August of 1880. In the meantime he and his brothers were finding success in buying and selling real estate, and getting into more trouble with the cowboys. Wyatt had a horse stolen from him and got a tipoff from an informer among the cowboys that Ike Clanton had it. Wyatt went after the horse and faced off against Ike. With Wyatt bluffing that a posse was on its way, Ike backed down and returned the horse.

The end of 1880 found Curley Bill out of jail. The Tucson judge ruled the killing had been accidental when the gun went off half-cocked. Both Wyatt and the dying Fred White had believed this to be the case. It did appear that Curley Bill felt real grief over White's death – not that it deterred him from his life of crime. While Wyatt would have liked nothing better than to see Curley Bill and his cowboy friends behind bars, he always told the truth in court.

Wyatt probably regretted his honesty. Once out of jail, Curley Bill promptly went on the mother of all sprees. After boozing it up with a friend, the two held up a dance hall and forced everyone to dance in the nude. When the law came, they shot their way out. Several horses got hit but the humans on both sides emerged unscathed. The next day, still drunk, Curley Bill stumbled into a church, ordered the preacher to stand perfectly still, and shot holes in the wall all around him. Then he forced him to dance. The day after that, he and his friends raced through Tombstone firing their pistols into the air, rode off to nearby Contention to rob a man of $50, and fired at the posse that came after him. Curley Bill then settled down to his usual activities of cattle rustling and robbing Mexican pack trains coming across the border. There was little the Mexicans could do, as the cowboys often picked on smugglers who couldn't go to the law.

On January 4, 1881, another election was held, this time for mayor. John Clum, editor of the *Epitaph*, won. This gave the Earps a powerful ally that they would rely on in the months to come.

In February of 1881, Tombstone increased in importance when it became the capital of the newly formed Cochise County. The territorial governor appointed Johnny Behan sheriff. Wyatt Earp expected Behan to appoint him undersheriff, which would have given him a good salary and a cut of the taxes. Behan had promised him the job, but picked Tombstone *Nugget* editor Harry Woods instead and never explained why. The Earps had lost out on yet another profitable position to a Democrat.

Not all of Arizona was barren desert. Mountain streams created hidden paradises for those lucky enough to know where they were. Here some soldiers and their female companions enjoy an outing sometime between 1884 and 1887. (LoC)

The bar at the Crystal Palace Saloon in Tombstone as it appeared *c.* 1885. It started in 1879 as the Golden Eagle Brewery saloon before changing its name. It was one of the more elegant drinking dens in the city and had a dining room serving delicacies such as oysters. The building still stands, and, after serving as a movie theater and later a ticket office for the town's Greyhound bus station, it is once again open as a bar and restaurant. (Arizona State Library, Archives and Public Records: History and Archives Division)

Behan proved quite effective at collecting taxes; he was even able to gather them from the rustlers by hiring Curley Bill to help. Behan's live-in girlfriend Josephine "Sadie" Marcus later wrote that the sheriff often invited Curley Bill along with Billy Clanton, Tom and Frank McLaury, and Johnny Ringo over for cards and private conversations.

By late 1880 and early 1881, law-abiding citizens were sick of the cowboys. The term had now become a universally derogatory one, and to call an honest drover a cowboy would invite a fight. Crime was on the rise, with the cowboys even murdering some of their victims. The last straw came on the night of March 15, 1881, when a stagecoach passed through Contention, a little mining settlement eight miles northwest of Tombstone that served as a base for the cowboys. Several men stepped out of the shadows and called for the stagecoach to stop. The guard, aspiring sheriff Bob Paul, pulled up his shotgun and shots were fired on both sides. The driver, a well-liked man named Bud Philpot, got hit and fell off dead. Another bullet crashed through the stagecoach to wound one of the passengers mortally. Paul grabbed the reins and whipped the horses down the road and to safety.

Sheriff Behan led a posse of the Earp brothers, Doc Holliday, Bat Masterson, and Wells Fargo agent Marshall Williams after the bandits. At the robbery site they found three masks made of twisted rope and a rope beard. The trail led to a ranch where they caught Luther King, who quickly admitted to having acted as horse holder for the bandits. He named his accomplices as Billy Leonard, Harry Head, and Jim Crane. No other evidence was found except a pair of fagged-out horses and a few dime novels. Wyatt Earp noticed one book was missing its back pages and carried it along. The trail continued to a recently vacated campsite where Wyatt found the rest of the book.

King was taken in but subsequently escaped by the ingenious method of walking out of the back door of the sheriff's office. This caused an outcry in the press and wide suspicion of collusion with the cowboys. Meanwhile Earp and the rest of the party searched for more than two weeks in the wilderness, while Behan did not send them supplies or fresh horses. He also failed to pay them, keeping the expenses billed to the county for himself.

People began to whisper that Doc Holliday had been one of the robbers. Billy Leonard was a gambling friend of Doc's and the dentist had hired a horse and ridden out of town a few hours before the robbery, only to come back at night with the horse completely worn out. Doc asserted that he returned by 6:30pm, well before the robbery, but witnesses claimed to have seen him galloping towards Tombstone right after the robbery. While the McLaury brothers and Ike Clanton were among their number – a fact that certainly didn't endear them to Doc – more neutral observers said the same thing.

Wyatt bristled under the implication of his friend's guilt, as it also brought suspicion upon himself and his brothers. He approached Ike Clanton and suggested the cowboy lure the robbers, who were friends of his, back to Tombstone so that he (Wyatt) could catch them. He would give Ike

SADIE MARCUS

Another factor in the tangled web of Tombstone politics was a beautiful and mysterious actress, Josephine "Sadie" Marcus (1861–December 20, 1944), who arrived in Arizona from San Francisco as part of an acting troupe. She had run away from her working-class home to find excitement in the Wild West. After engagements in Tucson, the troupe arrived in Tombstone on December 1, 1879, almost the exact time the Earps showed up.

Johnny Behan became enamored of her and, after a long suit, convinced Sadie to live with him as a common-law wife. Behan could not keep his attractions to one woman, however, and was soon running around with someone else. By the summer of 1881 Sadie was living on her own in Tombstone. Some old-timers recalled that she worked as a prostitute.

Soon Wyatt Earp became attracted to her. Wyatt was in an unhappy common-law marriage with former prostitute Celia Ann "Mattie" Blaylock. Mattie was addicted to laudanum and was becoming increasingly erratic. Sadie and Wyatt began to be seen together in public and this friendship blossomed into a romance that humiliated Behan and further widened the rift between him and the Earps.

Sadie stayed with Wyatt for the rest of his life, although times were hard. She became addicted to gambling, further exacerbating the couple's money issues. After Wyatt's death in 1929, Sadie devoted herself to protecting his memory. Mattie was written out of the story, as was most of Sadie's early life.

the reward and use the capture to help him win the sheriff position at the next election. Both Wyatt and Virgil later recounted that Ike agreed to the plan because he wanted Leonard's ranch. Ike, of course, denied all this, saying Wyatt and his friends were party to the robbery and wanted to bump off the bandits so they couldn't talk.

A cowboy photographed *c.* 1888 near Sturgis, Dakota Territory. While a long way from Arizona, cowboys up north needed the same equipment. Note the pistol at the belt, holstered with the butt facing the front for a crossdraw. This was the typical way to wear a pistol while riding. Note also the rifle in a scabbard, lariat, and chaps. A lariat was a length of rope used to lasso, hobble, and tie animals. Cowboys prided themselves on the skill with which they handled a rope and developed many tricks to show off at rodeos. Chaps were thick leather leggings that were essential for riding through underbrush, especially in the desert of the Southwest with its many cacti. (LoC)

Justice was served in a different way. Billy Leonard and Harry Head were killed by the brothers Ike and Bill Haslett for the reward money. The third stagecoach robber, Jim Crane, brought more than a dozen cowboys to hunt the Hasletts down. They found them along with another man, Sigman "Joe" Biertzhoff, in a New Mexico saloon. Nellie Pender was sitting on her porch nearby and heard the shots:

> I counted eight, but they say there were more. My husband started to run, but I caught hold of him and held him back until I heard them mount their horses and ride away like the wind. I ran and put out the light, and we started down ... The place was just running with blood. Bill Haslett was shot six times in his bowels, and Ike was shot through his head and his left hand was shot to pieces. The boy Joe was shot six times through his stomach and once through his ankle. He suffered the worst of any of them. They were all conscious to the last. The Haslett boys made out a will leaving everything to their father and sister in Kansas. The German boy's people live in California – he had nothing, not even enough to pay his debts in camp, but the company gave them all as good a funeral as could be had in this country. It was a sorrowful sight to see those three coffins followed by all the men moving slowly though camp.

The cowboys had become a force to be reckoned with.

The law was becoming a force to be reckoned with, too. In June of 1881, Virgil Earp was named city marshal to replace Ben Sippy, who had disappeared with many debts left unpaid. The cowboys now had a powerful enemy.

Opposite:
Cowboys from the Hash Knife ranch in Holbrook, Arizona Territory, *c.* 1890. This remarkable photograph shows the dress of the average rangemen of the time, the same as that of the rustlers who temporarily gave the term "cowboy" a bad name. Coats were generally not worn while working, the preference being for vests or sweaters depending on the weather. (Arizona State Library, Archives and Public Records: History and Archives Division)

1

GUNFIGHTERS OF THE OLD WEST

Gunfighters in the Old West were a varied lot. Some were simply bullies who had more aggressiveness than talent, while others truly studied their art. The more serious gunfighters had a variety of techniques and accessories to give them an edge in combat. It must be remembered that gunfights were fairly rare – even the famed Doc Holliday was only in one confirmed fight – but an edge could mean the difference between life and death.

(1) The Spin
This technique, also called the "road-agent's spin" or "Border roll," was a way for someone to appear to be surrendering while actually preparing to fire. Some scholars believe that Curley Bill Brocious used this on Sheriff Fred White in Tombstone on October 28, 1880.

The spin is performed in the following manner. The gunfighter offers his gun butt first to his opponent. The trigger finger is hooked inside the trigger guard and is not visible from straight ahead. The rest of the fingers cradle the gun's side and barrel. The gunfighter then jerks his hand upward. A well-balanced revolver will then spin around with the trigger finger as its axis and the butt of the revolver lands in the palm. The gun is now ready to fire.

It is unclear who invented the spin. John Wesley Hardin claimed to have used it on Abilene Marshal "Wild Bill" Hickock in 1871. This story appears in Hardin's self-serving 1895 autobiography and is open to question. Some sources claim the Innocents gang of Montana invented it as early as 1863.

(2) Fanning
Owners of a single-action revolver can get increased speed by using a method called "fanning." The gun is held in the dominant hand, usually at hip level where the forearm can be braced against the hip. The trigger is held in the firing position while the other hand repeatedly slaps the hammer, thus turning the cylinder and firing the bullets at a rapid rate.

This technique will not work on a double-action revolver because such a weapon requires the trigger to be pulled to turn the cylinder and fire a shot. Gunfighters preferred single-action revolvers even for regular shooting, because the extra effort required to pull the trigger of a double-action revolver could affect aim. Jesse James liked to use the Smith & Wesson Schofield .45. Like other gunfighters, he preferred single-action revolvers because with the hammer cocked, it only took a light pull on the trigger to fire.

3

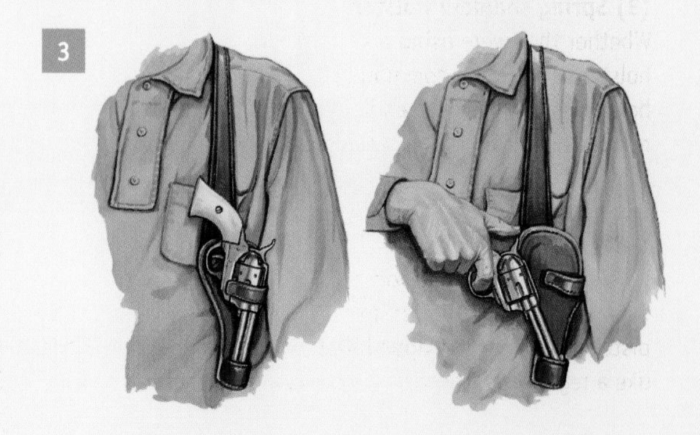

Fanning was rarely used in actual fights. It was more often used as a way of showing off. It also features in modern-day fast-draw competitions. Fanning did have some advantages in a fight situation, however. The sound and smoke lent a serious intimidation factor. If used against a cluster of opponents at close range, the gunman was likely to hit one or more of them and could get enough of a psychological drop on them to draw a second revolver and pick the survivors off more artfully.

At close range the black-powder revolver had another advantage. The blast itself lent an impact even if the bullet missed. The flare from the gun could even set a person's clothes or hair on fire. Five shots in rapid succession (no sane man carried six bullets in a single-action revolver) could easily send a small group of men into a stumbling panic.

(3) Spring shoulder holster

Whether they were using a shoulder holster or the more common belt holster, gunfighters generally cocked the revolver as they drew it, instead of waiting until they had the gun level. While waiting is the safer and more common practice, an experienced gunman wanted that extra split second.

Another way to shave off a tenth of a second or so was to have a spring shoulder holster. Instead of drawing the pistol, the gunman snapped it out of the holster. It looked like a regular holster with most of the front missing. The barrel rested in a leather toe while the cylinder was held lightly and firmly by a riveted cowhide spring clip. The gunman would cross draw. The forefinger would go into the trigger guard while the thumb pulled back the hammer and the other three fingers grabbed the butt and pulled the gun sideways. This made for a very fast draw.

Some gunmen preferred to protect their guns with a half-breed spring holster, which included the front flap. The side remained open but there was always the chance of catching the hand or the gun on that front flap.

(4) Bridgeport rig

The Bridgeport rig, sometimes called a "Gillett belt" after James Gillett, who wore one when he was marshal of El Paso in the 1880s, was a simple device that allowed a revolver to be fired without even being drawn.

A metal plate was riveted onto the belt; this plate had a slot open on the front end and with a depression at the back end. A special pin-headed screw was attached to the revolver, often replacing the regular hammer screw of a single-action Colt. This attachment was then inserted into the slot and pulled back until it fell into the depression at the back. The gun could be pivoted within the depression and fired from the hip.

The Bridgeport rig had the advantage that the gun could be fired while the gunman was sitting down, perhaps from under a table at someone who was cheating at cards.

Cowboys not only had to know how to handle a rope, a gun, and cattle, but also had to be experts on horses. A good steed was essential and it was equally important not to tire them out. Any good outfit kept plenty of spare horses, and on a cattle drive each cowboy rotated among six to ten horses. These cowboys at the Cheyenne River sometime between 1887 and 1892 are busy roping fresh horses to outfit them for the next shift. (LoC)

While Behan on one side and the Earps on the other represented leading figures in two opposing factions, neither was terribly popular. Many townsfolk mistrusted Behan for his suspected allegiance to the cowboys. The Earps were considered too dour by the fun-loving locals and many ranchers felt them to be too hard on the cowboys. A new breed of townspeople was making itself known as well. More and more cultured professionals from the East were arriving in Tombstone in search of new opportunities as the country struggled with a bad recession. They demanded law and order. They did not like Behan's dealings with desperadoes, nor the Earps dealing cards and living with former prostitutes. The Earps and Behan represented a divided region, where each side hated the other and was not terribly entranced with its own.

Just when the case of the stagecoach killings seemed to have run its course, with two suspects dead and the other gone to ground, it took a strange new twist. Doc Holliday's girlfriend, Big-Nose Kate, got angry with him and in a drunken rage accused him of being party to the holdup and murders. Behan gleefully arrested Holliday. The court found no evidence to support Kate's claims, nor could she provide any, so it threw out the case. That did not stop tongues from wagging. The story grew to encompass the Earp brothers as suspects too. In her memoirs, even Virgil's wife Allie said she felt certain the Earps and Holliday were in on the stagecoach robberies.

Meanwhile the exploits of the cowboys escalated, turning what was once a county problem into an international incident. The cowboys' robberies south of the border became more violent and the Mexicans began to strike back. When a group of cowboys stole several hundred head of cattle from the Vasquez ranch, the rancher and his men went after them and gunned them down. Vasquez was also killed in the gunfight. Sonora governor Luis Torres sent 200 soldiers to the border south of Cochise County in order to catch the next group of cowboys that came across.

An even bloodier incident occurred at about the same time, when a group of Mexicans was robbed and slaughtered in Skeleton Canyon, a popular smuggling route. The cowboys even killed a couple of Mexican soldiers riding back from Tombstone after buying supplies. Another cowboy raid into Mexico led to more stolen cattle. Some Mexican ranchers went after them and got the worst end of the fight, with eight killed.

Soon afterwards, at Guadalupe Canyon, another smuggling route across the border, a band of seven Americans was attacked as they slept on the American side of the line. Among the five dead were Jim Crane, the last stagecoach holdup suspect, and Old Man Clanton, head of the Clanton family. Crane had not even made it out of his sleeping roll. They had with them 100 head of cattle, although accounts vary as to whether they were stolen or legitimate. A survivor, who seems to have been an innocent ranch hand in the wrong place with the wrong people, testified they had been attacked by Mexican troops. Some suspected that the soldiers, tired of being limited to the south of the border, had slipped across the line to take care of what the gringos would not. Rumors spread that the cowboys had gathered a group of 200 desperadoes to attack Mexico, and that the Mexican army was gearing up to repel the invasion. The national press in the U.S.A. began to take serious notice of events in southern Arizona.

Many felt the cowboys had gotten what they deserved. George Parsons wrote in his diary:

> This killing business by the Mexicans, in my mind, was perfectly justifiable as it was in retaliation for killing of several of them and their robbery by cow-boys recently this same Crane being one of the number. Am glad they killed him, as for the others – if not guilty of cattle stealing – they had no business to be found in such bad company.

There were rumors that there had been other gunfights. The English newspaper *Graphic Illustrated* reported in its November 26, 1881 issue that Curley Bill

> ... and another named M'Allister went into Mexico, and actually drove out three hundred head of cattle. They were pursued by a body of Mexicans, and overtaken in Arizona about thirty miles from Galeyville, at a place where stood an old abandoned house. The pursuers having secured their cattle, "went for" the cow-boys. Curley Bill and his companion had taken possession of the deserted house, and they held it against the Mexicans. The siege was maintained for three days, and the two men had neither food nor water all that time. Their plight was very desperate, when some of their comrades came by chance that way. The Mexicans then deemed it the better part of valor to retire, but they left twelve dead bodies behind them. During the hostilities Curley Bill was shot in the head in three places, but M'Allister's damage consisted only of a flesh-wound in the neck. Curley Bill recovered, but after that it was noticed that when the worse of liquor he seemed a bit crazy, and people kept out of his way. When sober, however, he was considered all right. Some little time after his accident he was in Tombstone, a mining town, and got drunk. The "Marshal," anglicé policeman, thought then to arrest him, but Curly Bill shot him dead on the spot.

While this article was probably as much journalistic imagination as true reportage, Curley Bill was certainly making a reputation for himself. He, Ike Clanton, and Johnny Ringo began to be noted as the ringleaders of an organized gang. Exactly how much of a real gang it was remains a matter of debate. Many historians believe the organization and unity of the cowboys to have been exaggerated in the contemporary press and later histories.

The exploits of its leaders were certainly exaggerated. Ringo, for instance, has been portrayed as an educated gentleman gunfighter fond of speaking in Latin. Some writers even claimed he was a university professor turned bad. In fact Ringo had only a basic education, having grown up in poverty in California. When he was 14, he and his family set out in a wagon train from Missouri to the coast. He witnessed his father's accidental death one morning when the man stepped out of the wagon with a shotgun in hand and it went off. One eyewitness said, "At the report of his gun I saw his hat blown up 20 feet in the air and his brains were scattered in all directions. I never saw a more heartrending sight, and to see the distress and agony of his wife and children was painful in the extreme."

This childhood trauma may have led to his alcoholism and mean streak. He stood a hefty 6ft 3in. and people noted that he had a certain charisma and force of will. Everyone considered him dangerous, and he was. He was a veteran of the Mason County Range Wars in Texas, where he killed at least two men. Like many of the unusual figures on the Frontier, he also acted on

CHARLIE SMITH

Origen "Charlie" Smith (1849/50–1907), a native of Indiana, was, like the Earps, both a gambler and a lawman. He had the cruel nickname of "Harelip Charlie" due to a birth defect that, unlike Doc Holliday, he never had fixed.

It is unclear when or why Smith headed West. He tended bar and got into shootouts for a while in Fort Worth, Texas, and proved himself more hot-headed than accurate; there is no record that he ever killed anyone. When reform fever hit the town in late 1878, causing a number of saloon closures, Smith headed to the more permissive climate of Arizona. He was soon filing mining claims in Tombstone. Smith already knew Jim Earp and became good friends with Wyatt, who backed him on a number of ventures. He had little luck with mining, however, and had to make ends meet as a gambler.

Smith was good friends with Fred Dodge, whom he had known in his Texas days, and rode with the Earps on several of their posses. Smith also contributed to Wyatt's and Doc's bail money after the gunfight at the O.K. Corral. He was one of the Earp supporters who rushed to the scene when Morgan was fatally shot. Smith joined the Vendetta Ride and left with them for Colorado after it was finished.

Smith later returned to Tombstone and became a deputy sheriff under two of Behan's successors. Dodge was also a lawman at this time and together they rode after rustlers and train robbers. Smith's luck ran out when he tried to stop a fight at the Bank Exchange Saloon in Tombstone on November 25, 1885. A drunken onlooker, Charles Cunningham, butted in and called Smith a "damned harelip son of a bitch." Taking exception to that, Smith shot him in the leg. Cunningham never forgot this and the two got into it again on September 22, 1888. First they tussled at the French Wine House, and later Cunningham got a pistol and hunted Smith down in the street. His shot shattered Smith's hip-bone. Recovery was slow and painful, but Smith served in various law-enforcement roles in Tempe and Maricopa, Arizona, until his death in 1907.

the right side of the law, briefly serving as constable in Loyal Valley, Mason County, in 1878. Roles were rarely clear-cut on the edge of civilization. A year later he moved to Arizona. One of his first acts was to shoot a man in the head for refusing to drink whiskey with him. The fellow said he preferred beer and Ringo apparently found that insulting.

During the fall and winter of 1881 the stagecoach robberies continued. The Earps arrested Frank Stilwell and Pete Spence, two cowboys, for one of the jobs, and some other cowboys, including Ike Clanton, cornered Morgan Earp in the street and threatened his life.

The cowboys were not only robbing stagecoaches, but also rustling from big American ranches. The Mexican army was guarding the border more vigilantly and so opportunities had dried up south of the line. The Cattlegrowers Association put a $1,000 bounty on Curley Bill's head and a vigilance committee formed in town. With Tombstone's lawmen spending as much time sparring with each other as they did fighting criminals, ordinary citizens got ready to take the law into their own hands.

Meanwhile, Ike Clanton was still worried that his secret dealings with the Earps to capture the stagecoach robbers would be revealed. A cowboy ratting out his fellow cowboys would not have long to live. Ike got it into his head that Wyatt had told Doc Holliday. The dentist was such a busy gambler that he was acquainted with many of the cowboys. In Ike's mind he was the worst person who could know. Ike pestered Wyatt so much about the matter that Wyatt sent Morgan up to Tucson to fetch Holliday. They returned October 22, 1881. The stage was set and all the actors were upon it.

OCTOBER 22, 1881

Doc Holliday returns to Tombstone from Tucson

Ike Clanton, c. 1880, when he was about 33 years old. Far from being a grizzled, dirty cowboy as he has been represented in some movies, Ike was a prosperous rancher and could afford to dress well, although his income came from less-than-honest sources. (Arizona State Library, Archives and Public Records: History and Archives Division)

THE GUNMEN

Things were coming to a head. Everyone in Tombstone realized the Earps and the cowboys would end up in a showdown sooner or later. What is remarkable about later testimony about the gunfight at the O.K. Corral is that while everyone was shocked, few were very much surprised.

There was no grand strategy or overall plan. This was by no means a military operation, even though several of the people involved were veterans. While everyone knew a fight was brewing, nobody knew exactly when it would happen. This is not to say that Wyatt Earp and his followers were unprepared. The Earps had come to Tombstone to settle and grow rich. They established themselves in positions of influence. As tensions with the cowboys mounted, they were careful to create strong ties with those who could help them.

The strongest ties were with an unlikely source – the drinkers and gamblers who frequented the Oriental. In her memoirs, Allie Earp said the Oriental had a bad reputation and that was certainly true. It was considered a rough place and there was no shortage of fights there. The men who lounged around the faro tables were hotheaded, opinionated, and loyal to their friends. These were exactly the kind of people the Earps needed. Some of them, such as Turkey Creek Jack Johnson, Texas Jack Vermillion, and Charlie Smith, were old friends. Some had been called up for work as special deputies. The Earps were careful to foster relationships with these people, helping them out in business and with their frequent run-ins with the law.

The Earp faction was not the only group to frequent the Oriental. It was a cowboy hangout as well. It is remarkable that both factions frequently played cards together, even on the night before the gunfight at the O.K. Corral. To many observers, there was little difference between the two groups. One eyewitness to the famous gunfight told his father, "This is nothing but a bunch of stage-robbers splitting, and killing one another to keep any evidence from getting out."

Weapons

Fictional narratives of the Old West tend to focus on the six-shooter revolver, that universal symbol of manhood on the Frontier. In the O.K. Corral and subsequent Vendetta Ride, however, shotguns and rifles were used just as much.

Two rifles are mentioned frequently in the source material – the Henry and the Winchester. The Henry rifle was a lever-action, breech-loading rifle that fired .44-caliber rimfire cartridges. Produced by the New Haven Arms Company starting in 1860, it saw widespread use by Union soldiers during the Civil War. It had a 16-round tube magazine and thus offered much more firepower than the muzzleloaders issued by the armies of both sides. Production stopped in 1866 when the company came out with the Winchester Model 1866. In that year the company changed its name to the Winchester Repeating Arms Company. While there are frequent mentions of Henry rifles in the accounts of the Arizona War, these must be treated with caution. By the 1880s most Henry rifles would have been replaced by the newer and better Winchesters, especially considering that the men on both sides were relatively well off and relied on their guns for their livelihood. It may be that the old name for the rifle stuck, and that when some people said "Henry rifle," they were in fact referring to later Winchesters.

The Winchester Model 1866 was an improvement on the Henry rifle, but kept the same basic design. Improvements included a redesigned magazine to keep out dirt and a wooden forearm stock to prevent powder burns. Instead of loading from the rear as with the Henry rifle, loading was done from the side. The Winchester Model 1873 switched to a more powerful .44-40 centerfire cartridge. Variants could take .32-20 or .38-40 ammunition. All three were popular handgun calibers and thus a man could carry the same ammunition for both his rifle and his pistol. Both models had a 15-round tube magazine. The Model 1873 was produced as a rifle, carbine, and more rarely a smoothbore. The Model 1873 was hugely popular on the Frontier, especially the carbine, which came with a shorter barrel and proved easier to handle on horseback. Another rifle was the Winchester Model 1876, which used full-power centerfire cartridges of various calibers but larger than the standard pistol ammunition used by the Model 1873. The Model 1876 was popular with buffalo hunters for its stopping power.

Shotguns came in various makes and models in the 1880s. They were generally double-barreled and loaded with buckshot. As would be proven with the attempted murder of Virgil Earp and the gunfight at Iron Springs, they were effective even from medium range and the spray of pellets proved a handy remedy to the notorious inaccuracy of the revolvers of the period.

As for revolvers, the most popular at this time was the Colt Frontier Six-Shooter, also called "the Peacemaker." The Model 1873 was 11in. long with a 5.5in. barrel, or 13in. long with a 7.5in. barrel. It used a .44-40 centerfire cartridge interchangeable with the Winchester rifle model that came out that same year. Another popular model was the Colt Single Action Army, which fired a .45-caliber bullet. Wyatt Earp is also known to have owned a .44-caliber 1869 American model Smith & Wesson, given to him by *Epitaph* editor John Clum.

Virgil Earp in a photograph said to have been taken c. 1881 when he was a lawman in Tombstone. The oldest of the three Earp brothers active in law enforcement, Virgil would have been approaching 40 at the time this photograph was taken. (Arizona Historical Society, photo #1444)

Pistols made for handy non-lethal weapons through the frequent practice of pistol-whipping, called "buffaloing" in the slang of the time as mentioned earlier. This could be done either by cracking someone over the head with a downward motion, bringing the sharp lower end of the grip down on the top of the skull, or by the more common method of slapping someone upside the head with the pistol barrel. While some researchers assert that Wyatt Earp used his Model 1869 S&W at the O.K. Corral, others point out that earlier in the day he hit Tom McLaury across the face with his pistol. The cylinder of the Model 1869 can pop out if it is given a sharp shock to the side. Thus it is unlikely that Wyatt would have buffaloed Tom with a Smith & Wesson.

Popular accounts have long said that Wyatt Earp carried a pistol called a Colt Buntline Special. This specially made .45 single-action revolver had a 12in. barrel and a shoulder stock, thus converting it into a carbine. It was supposedly created by the Colt company in a limited edition of five, ordered by dime novelist Ned Buntline and presented to Wyatt Earp and four other Dodge City lawmen in the summer of 1876. Modestly, the writer named this gun the "Buntline Special" after himself. The story was originally told in the oft-cited but error-ridden *Wyatt Earp: Frontier Marshal* by Stuart Lake. The problem is, there is no evidence that it ever happened. No contemporary account mentions this remarkable weapon and Colt has no record of such a sale. Also, Ned Buntline was not even in Kansas that year. The story appears to have been one of the many made up by Stuart Lake.

Equipment

Frontiersmen spared their horses by keeping their equipment to a minimum. Besides their weapons, they would carry only a large canteen, bedroll, basic provisions, and a mess kit. Cowboys would, of course, carry a lariat for catching steers, but during the Vendetta Ride there would have been no use for this.

People could travel light because they could rely on the locals. The Arizona countryside was not empty. In the valleys were scattered ranches and in the hills were mining and timber camps. Hospitality was universal. A traveler would think nothing of knocking on a stranger's door and asking for food and shelter. The homeowner would rarely turn someone away, although it was considered polite for the guest to offer some work or some small payment. Using a rancher's well did not even require asking permission.

Some sources state that Charlie Smith drove a wagon full of supplies during the Vendetta Ride. This would have proven useful if the men wanted to stay out in the wilderness for long periods of time. News traveled fast on the Frontier, and the law was after Wyatt and his friends. While they availed themselves of local hospitality from time to time, it also made sense to keep their contact with the public to a minimum.

Some assert that Wyatt Earp owned a bulletproof vest and wore it at the gunfight at Iron Springs. This was relayed by a few sources, including Big-Nose Kate and two cowboys who claimed to have been at the fight. Wyatt vigorously denied that he ever owned one and in fact it makes little sense. This author has spent many a hot day hiking and riding around southern Arizona and can testify that the idea of wearing a bulletproof vest, especially of the clunky 19th-century variety, is unthinkable. The danger of heat prostration would offset any sort of safety it might provide. It is important to note that all parties to the battle said that the fight came as a complete surprise to everyone. Wyatt was not expecting a gunfight, and would not have been wearing a bulletproof vest all day even if he owned one.

THE RAID

The O.K. Corral

In the small hours of October 26, 1881, Doc Holliday and Morgan Earp bumped into Ike Clanton at the Occidental Lunch Room, part of the Alhambra Saloon. Holliday was drunk as usual and loudly berated Ike, saying he was a damned liar for accusing Wyatt of betraying a trust, and calling Ike a "son of a bitch of a cowboy." The drunken, violent dentist was very protective of his few friends. This did not exactly reassure Ike Clanton that his secret was safe and he started to verbally abuse Holliday. According to Ike, Doc put his hand inside his shirt, a favorite holdout place for a gun, and urged Ike to have a shootout with him. When Ike replied that he wasn't armed, Doc replied, "You son of a bitch, if you ain't heeled [armed], go and heel yourself." Ike said that Morgan joined in on the taunts and Ike simply walked away. In the Earp version of events, Morgan stepped in to break up the argument before it escalated into anything worse. Ike later buttonholed Wyatt: "He told me when Holliday approached him in the Alhambra that he wasn't fixed just right. He said that in the morning he would have man-for-man, that this fighting talk had been going on for a long time and he guessed it was about time to fetch it to a close." Ike reportedly finished off with the threat that "I'll be ready for you all in the morning." Wyatt said of his reply, "I told him I would not fight no one if I could get away from it, because there was no money in it."

Despite Ike and probably most of the others being drunk and angry, he and Virgil Earp, Tom McLaury, Johnny Behan, and some innocent fellow whose name has been lost to history sat down for an all-night poker game. When Virgil got up at 7am to go home, Ike told him to tell Holliday that "the damned son of a bitch has got to fight." Virgil said he was going to bed and didn't want to be woken up for any trouble. Ike called after him, "You won't carry the message?" When Virgil said no, Ike called out, "You may have to fight before you know it."

Virgil did not reply and went home. His wife Allie was up and asked him how the evening had gone. Virgil replied that he had been trying to keep Holliday and Ike from murdering each other. "Why didn't you let them go ahead?" she snapped. "Neither one amounts to much."

Ike continued to drink and brag about what he'd do to Doc and the Earps. As early as 8am a bartender noticed he was armed. This man went to Wyatt's home and woke him up to warn him, but the gunfighter simply rolled over and went back to sleep. Wyatt never took Ike very seriously. Ike continued his bar crawl and rumors of an imminent fight spread through town. Someone told Virgil but he showed as little concern as his brother.

Later that morning Ike appeared at Holliday's abode, Fly's Boarding House, with a pistol and a Winchester rifle, demanding to see him. He was turned away and Doc was warned. The gunfighter quickly got dressed and readied his weapons. Wyatt Earp was also up, and heard that Ike was hunting for him and his friends.

Ike Clanton's boasts wouldn't last out the morning. At noon Virgil spotted him in the street with a pistol stuffed into his belt and a Winchester in his hand. Virgil snuck up behind him and grabbed the rifle with his left hand. When Ike turned and tried to draw his revolver, Virgil smacked him on the side of the head with the barrel of his pistol and sent him to his knees. As Virgil told the court later, "I asked him if he was hunting for me. He said he was, and if he saw me a second sooner he would have killed me. I arrested Ike for carrying firearms, I believe was the charge, inside city limits."

HARPER'S WEEKLY
A JOURNAL OF CIVILIZATION
NEW YORK, SATURDAY, APRIL

Camillus Sydney Fly had the dubious distinction of having the gunfight at the O.K. Corral happen right outside his photographic studio. While he didn't take photos of that event, Fly did produce numerous historic shots of the Southwest, not the least of which was of Geronimo's surrender in 1886. Geronimo was an Apache leader who first went on the warpath when Mexican soldiers killed his mother, wife, and three children in 1858. Along with a band of warriors, he continued to resist the theft of Apache land for nearly 30 years, fighting against Mexican and U.S. authorities. (LoC)

This last detail is significant. There was an ordinance against carrying guns in Tombstone. Ike had been talking violence against the Earps and Holliday for almost 12 hours and flourishing guns for at least four hours and Virgil was the first person to do anything about it. This shows just how much the cowboy faction could get away with flouting the law.

Virgil hauled the sore-headed Ike to the Cochise County courthouse, left him in custody of Special Deputy Morgan, and went in search of the judge. While he was gone, Wyatt and an ever-growing crowd of spectators showed up. The crowd included people from both factions as well as regular townsfolk. Wyatt and Morgan took turns taunting Ike, offering to give him a gun and pay his bail if he'd fight. Ike seethed but didn't take the bait.

Judge Wallace appeared, settled things down, and gave Ike a fine of $25 plus court fees. Fellow cowboy Billy Claiborne then took Ike to the doctor to have his head seen to. As everyone filed out of the courtroom, Tom McLaury appeared and faced off with Wyatt. What words were exchanged

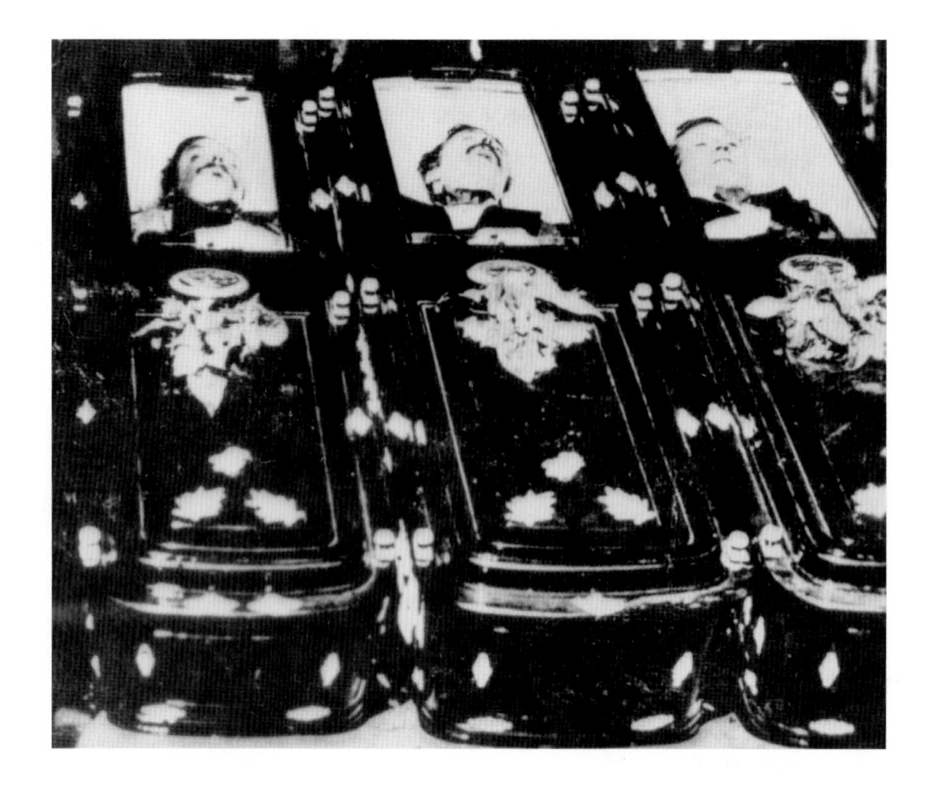

The aftermath of the O.K. Corral gunfight. From left to right, Tom McLaury, Frank McLaury, and Billy Clanton lie in fine caskets before being buried on Boot Hill in Tombstone. (Arizona State Library, Archives and Public Records: History and Archives Division)

is unclear. Witnesses say Wyatt slapped him and asked if he was armed. Tom replied that he wasn't. Then Wyatt pulled out his revolver and hit Tom with it before stalking off to buy a cigar. At the inquest after the O.K. Corral fight, Wyatt claimed Tom was armed, but at least three eyewitnesses said he wasn't. Although Wyatt had been goaded by the cowboys numerous times, this was a plain case of bullying.

As all this was happening, Frank McLaury and Billy Clanton rode into town, being greeted cordially by Doc Holliday, who was now prowling the streets. The two cowboys went for a drink at the Grand Hotel and while at the bar they were told about the morning's events. Frank was heard to say, "I will get the boys out of town. We won't drink." Frank and Billy headed back to get their horses from the O.K. Corral.

On their way they met Billy Claiborne fresh from the doctor's office. They repeated their words of wanting to get everyone out of town. Soon afterwards the McLaurys and Clanton were seen at Spangenberg's Gun Shop buying ammunition. They may have wanted to avoid a fight, but they wanted to be prepared for one, too. Ike appeared and tried to buy a pistol but the shopkeeper wisely refused to sell him one.

Wyatt spotted them. He watched for a while and then saw Frank McLaury's horse wander up the sidewalk. Apparently the cowboy was so rattled he had forgotten to hitch his mount properly. The animal got up on the wooden sidewalk and poked his head into the gun shop in search of its master. Wyatt strolled over, took the bit, and led the horse out. The cowboys rushed to the door and Wyatt coolly informed them that they had to keep the horse off the sidewalk.

John Clum posing with Native Americans in the Buehman Studios, Tucson, c. 1877 when he was about 26 years old. Clum served as Indian agent for the San Carlos Apache Indian Reservation in the Arizona Territory from 1874 to 1877. He was known for his fair treatment of peaceful Indians, offering more self-rule and fighting corruption in the U.S. Army and Indian Bureau. He fought renegade Indians as well, capturing Geronimo on April 21, 1877. It is likely this photo is in celebration of that event. (Arizona State Library, Archives and Public Records: History and Archives Division)

The cowboys weren't the only ones arming themselves. Virgil picked up his shotgun from the Wells Fargo office. As the cowboys left the gun shop and collected their mounts at the O.K. Corral, Virgil, Wyatt, and Morgan Earp, plus Doc Holliday, met at the corner of Fourth and Allen. Several people warned them the cowboys were at the corral ready for trouble. A member of the local vigilance committee offered 25 men to help, but Virgil said that as long as the cowboys stayed in the corral and not the street, he'd leave them alone. The technicality of the gun ordinance was that you could carry a gun if you were entering or leaving town, or if you were in a corral, these businesses being the usual places where people left their arms while doing business in town.

Were the cowboys planning on leaving or were they gearing up for a fight? This has been hotly disputed ever since that chilly October day. Perhaps the strongest evidence in favor of the fight theory comes from the account of train engineer H. F. Sills, who had arrived in town only the day before. He knew none of the people involved. As he stood on Fremont Street, Sills

> ... saw four or five men standing in front of the O.K. Corral ... talking of some trouble they had with Virgil Earp, and they made threats at the time, that on meeting him they would kill him on sight. Some one of the party spoke up at the time and said that they would kill the whole party of Earps when they met them.

When Sills asked a local who this fellow named Virgil Earp was, he was told he was the city marshal. Sills then hunted down Virgil and told him what he

The wooden grave markers at Boot Hill have been repainted countless times. This is one of the most photographed, even though the McLaurys were buried in a double grave separately from Billy Clanton. (LoC)

thought was shocking news. Virgil must have been amused at this newcomer's breathless announcement. More serious was the information from a local that the cowboys had left the corral and were now standing in a vacant lot on the edge of Fremont Street. They were now in contravention of the law against bearing arms. Virgil decided to arrest them.

Virgil and his group all had revolvers in holsters or tucked into their belts or pockets. To appear less threatening, Virgil gave Doc his shotgun and held Doc's walking stick in his right hand, his shooting hand. Virgil would do the talking and try to defuse the situation while the others would be backup in case of trouble.

Sheriff Behan now appeared on the scene, approaching the Clantons and McLaurys as they stood in the vacant lot next to the O.K. Corral. Popular legend and far too many Hollywood movies have this lot right next to Fly's Photographic Studio. In fact it was next to Fly's Boarding House, with the studio just behind it. This boarding house just happened to be where Doc Holliday lived. Why the cowboys were in this lot rather than in the corral has never been explained. Perhaps they hoped Doc would come home alone. Only Frank McLaury and Billy Clanton had their horses with them.

Behan later claimed not to have seen any weapons on Ike Clanton and Tom McLaury. He told the rest that he wanted to disarm them, but Frank McLaury replied that he wouldn't give up his weapons unless Behan disarmed the Earps and Holliday. The sheriff was standing on Fremont Street while the cowboys were standing in the lot out of sight. Behan spotted the Earps and Holliday coming down the street and hurried to meet them.

"Gentlemen," Behan said. "I am sheriff of this county, and I am not going to allow any trouble, if I can help it." The four gunfighters walked right by him and he followed, saying, "For God's sake, don't go down there or you will get murdered."

"I am going to disarm them," Virgil told him. "I have disarmed them all," Behan replied, contradicting what he had said a moment before about them getting murdered. Still the four did not stop. An eyewitness heard one of the Earps tell Holliday, "Let them have it," and the dentist replied, "All right." Behan trailed them and as they approached the lot, he took cover near the door to Fly's Boarding House at the edge of the vacant lot.

The cowboys spotted them. Billy Claiborne, who had never been looking for a fight, walked over to Behan. The Clantons and McLaurys edged back into the lot. As the Earps and Holliday entered the lot, they saw the four standing in a line. For a moment nobody moved, nobody drew.

"Boys, throw up your hands, I want your guns," Virgil commanded. He raised his right hand with the walking stick high. Billy Clanton and Frank McLaury drew their revolvers and cocked them as they drew. Ike Clanton put his hand in an opening in his open shirtfront. "Hold on, I don't want that," Virgil said as he threw both hands in the air.

It is unclear what exactly happened next and the sequence of events has been disputed ever since. The generally held theory is that two shots went off as Billy Clanton and Wyatt Earp fired almost simultaneously. The cowboys said both shots were from the Earp side. Frank McLaury staggered back with a bullet in the belly but remained standing. There was a second's silence. Virgil changed his walking stick from his right hand to his left and

Gunfight at the O.K. Corral (overleaf)

This scene shows a moment approximately halfway through the gunfight at the O.K. Corral. The fight actually took place in an open lot behind the O.K. Corral, between the Harwood House and Fly's Boarding House and Photo Gallery. Virgil Earp, accompanied by brothers Wyatt and Morgan plus Doc Holliday, had marched down Fremont Street to the lot where Ike and Billy Clanton, Frank and Tom McLaury, and Billy Claiborne were gathered. Virgil intended on disarming them after they had spent hours threatening the Earp group.

After failing to defuse the situation, Virgil Earp has been shot through the calf and has fallen to the ground. In his left hand he still holds his walking stick while in his right he is firing a pistol at Billy Clanton. Morgan Earp has also been hit and stumbles over a ridge in the ground made by a water pipe. Wyatt Earp stands nearby, unhurt and firing at Billy Clanton. Billy Clanton has been hit numerous times and has backpedaled until ramming into the wall of the Harwood House. He is slowly sinking to the ground but still fighting. He has been hit in the right wrist but has enough presence of mind to do a "border shift," tossing his pistol to his left hand so that he can continue firing.

Tom McLaury, having been hit in the armpit by Doc Holliday's shotgun blast, is staggering mortally wounded into the street as his horse gallops away. Doc Holliday has used up both barrels of his shotgun, dropped it, and is drawing a pistol to go after the wounded Frank McLaury, who is using his horse as cover while he tries to make his getaway on the street.

After the silver mines closed and the investors looked elsewhere, Tombstone was in danger of becoming a ghost town, like so many other boomtowns of the American West. It was saved from this fate by its reputation, which the townspeople capitalized on for the emerging tourist market. This sign stood outside town in 1937 and was meant to lure motorists with tales of Western gunfights. Famous Depression-era photographer Dorothea Lange captured some more local flavor by waiting for two Mexicans on a burro (small donkey) to pass by. (LoC)

drew his revolver. Billy Clanton's horse reared as Tom McLaury struggled to get the rifle from its scabbard.

Then shots came from all sides as everyone opened up. Holliday edged around Tom and the horse and blasted him under the armpit. The impact made Tom stagger into the street.

Ike Clanton threw his arms in the air and raced for Wyatt, screaming that he was unarmed. Wyatt growled, "The fight has commenced. Go to fighting or get away." He shoved the cowboy out of the way and Ike continued running for two city blocks before he stopped.

Virgil fell down with a shot to the calf, probably fired by Billy Clanton. Morgan shot Billy Clanton in the chest, wrist, and stomach. Far more game than his brother Ike, Billy backpedaled and switched hands in a move called a "border shift." His backpedaling ended when he hit the wall of Harwood's house. He slid to the ground, still firing.

Morgan fell, and cried out that he was hit. Meanwhile, Holliday dropped the shotgun and drew his revolver.

Wincing from his wound, Frank McLaury pushed his horse toward Fremont Street, using the animal as cover and firing at Morgan as he went. McLaury's horse bolted, leaving him exposed and squatting in the street.

Holliday stalked towards him. Frank McLaury raised his weapon. "I have got you now," Frank said. "Blaze away. You're a daisy if you have,"

Doc taunted him. Frank fired, grazing Doc in the hip and causing him to shout, "I'm shot right through!"

Frank got up and started to move. Morgan and Doc took shots at him and both hit, Morgan putting a bullet in his head and Doc hitting his chest. The smoke cleared to show Frank lying in the dirt, still moving. Holliday approached him yelling, "The son of a bitch has shot me, and I mean to kill him!"

Farther away, Tom McLaury was breathing his last at the base of a telegraph pole at the corner of Third and Fremont. Billy Clanton was the only one left with some fight in him. He feebly tried to reload his pistol only to be disarmed by Mr Fly, the photographer, who emerged from his studio into the smoke-wreathed air to put a final end to the shootout. It was all over. It had taken about 30 seconds.

While Virgil and Holliday had only been lightly wounded, Morgan was seriously hurt. A bullet had pierced his shoulder, chipped a vertebra, and exited his other shoulder. It is unclear if this happened before he fell, if it made him fall, or if he was shot after he fell. Some assert that he actually tripped over the hump of earth caused by a partially submerged water main.

As acrid gun smoke hung in the air, the shrill sound of a steam whistle shrieked from a nearby mine. It sounded a second time, and dozens of armed men emerged from their homes and businesses and met at predetermined points. They were members of a vigilance committee, known to many and whispered about in rumors by all. The sound of gunfire on the streets of Tombstone had set off the alarm. As news spread about what had happened, the men of the vigilance committee applauded the Earps and Holliday.

Early silent Western star Tom Mix posed in this publicity shot for his 1918 film *Mr. Logan, U.S.A.* In real life Mix had a colorful career, serving as sheriff of Dewey, Oklahoma, in 1904 and working in traveling Wild West shows before going to Hollywood and becoming one of its biggest stars. He was a great admirer of Wyatt Earp and attended his funeral. (LoC)

Visitors to modern Tombstone can see a variety of sideshows to take them back to the "good old days," including this animatronic gunfight at the O.K. Corral, in which the figures creak through the motions of the gunfight as a crackly recorded soundtrack of unenthusiastic actors goes through the lines supposedly said on that fateful day. (David Lee Summers)

Meanwhile Billy Clanton and Tom McLaury were carried into a house and made comfortable. Frank McLaury had already died on the street. A doctor was called to deal with the two wounded cowboys and declared their wounds fatal. Tom McLaury had a dozen buckshot wounds in a small cluster on his side. When the coroner went through his effects, he made the interesting statement that he found no guns or cartridges. Some witnesses said that at the beginning of the confrontation, Tom had opened his coat and declared he wasn't armed.

While Tom died without speaking a word, Billy Clanton was still all too conscious. Writhing in pain, he called for morphine and cried out, "They have murdered me. I have been murdered. Chase the crowd away from the door and give me air." A doctor gave him morphine and he slipped into a sleep from which he never awoke.

As this was going on, Wyatt directed some onlookers to help Virgil and Morgan to their homes. Sheriff Behan came up to him and declared, "I will have to arrest you."

"I won't be arrested," Wyatt replied. "You deceived me, Johnny, you told me they were not armed. I won't be arrested, but I am here to answer what I have done. I am not going to leave town."

While the Earps escaped jail, Ike Clanton did not. He was found a couple of blocks away and put behind bars under heavy guard.

The initial reaction to the gunfight was generally positive. An editorial in the *Epitaph* the next day said:

> The feeling among the best class of our citizens is that the Marshal was entirely justified in his efforts to disarm these men, and that being fired upon they had to defend themselves, which they did most bravely. So long as our peace officers make effort to preserve the peace and put down highway robbery – which the Earp brothers have done, having engaged in the pursuit and capture, where capture have been made of every gang of stage robbers in the county – they will have the support of all good citizens. If the present lesson is not sufficient to teach the cow-boy element that they cannot come into the streets of Tombstone, in broad daylight, armed with six-shooters and Henry rifles to hunt down their victims, then the citizens will most assuredly take such steps to preserve the peace as will be forever a bar to further raids.

Newspapers across the region and as far away as San Francisco, home to many of Arizona's mining investors, heralded the Earps as heroes.

It was not to last. Two days after the gunfight, the cowboys gathered to bury their dead. The bodies were displayed in front of the funeral parlor with a sign reading "MURDERED IN THE STREETS OF TOMBSTONE." An estimated 300 people turned out for the funeral. The dead cowboys were dressed in suits and placed in caskets with silver trimming. A brass band led a procession numbering more than 300 to the graveyard. Clara Brown wrote in the *San Diego Union*:

> A stranger viewing the funeral cortege, which was the largest ever seen in Tombstone, would have thought that some person esteemed by the entire camp was being conveyed to his final resting place ... such a public manifestation of sympathy from so large a portion of the residents of the camp seemed reprehensible when it is remembered that the deceased were nothing more or less than thieves ... The divided state of society in Tombstone is illustrated by this funeral ... Opinion is pretty fairly divided as to the justification of the killing. You may meet one man who will support the Earps, and declare that no other course was possible to save their own lives, and the next man is just as likely to assert that there was no occasion whatever for bloodshed, and that this will be "a warm place" for the Earps hereafter.

The coroner's inquest opened on October 28 with some damning testimony against the Earps and Holliday. Behan testified that Billy Clanton had shouted, "Don't shoot me, I don't want to fight!" and that Tom McLaury opened his coat and said, "I have got nothing." Ike Clanton and Billy Claiborne testified that none of the cowboys went for their guns and that Morgan Earp and Doc Holliday shot first. They agreed with Behan's testimony that Tom McLaury had thrown open his coat and said he was unarmed, and that Billy Clanton and Frank McLaury had their hands in the air. Pending further investigation, the city council suspended Virgil and temporarily replaced him with part-time policeman Jim Flynn. Ike Clanton filed murder charges against the Earps and Holliday. Justice of the Peace Wells Spicer fixed bail at $10,000 apiece. This was a huge sum for that time but the Earp faction had no trouble raising it.

Meanwhile, the cowboys were raising their own funds to hire a team of lawyers for the upcoming preliminary hearing. The Earps hired an attorney as well and Tombstone became entranced with the details of a long and complex hearing. It is beyond the scope of this book to go into detail about the proceedings. Numerous witnesses were called and the picture that emerged is a confusing one. Behan repeated his claim that the Earp side fired the first two shots almost immediately after Virgil had ordered the cowboys to surrender. He observed that the first shot was from a nickel-plated pistol. Behan could not recall for certain that it was Holliday's pistol, but said that he believed it was his. Billy Claiborne

Modern actors recreate the gunfight at the O.K. Corral in Tombstone every day. (David Lee Summers)

A Wells Fargo Express Co. treasure wagon shipping $250,000 gold bullion from the Great Homestake Mine, Deadwood, South Dakota, in 1890. When Wells Fargo began to lose its near-monopoly on shipping to express train services, it began to serve more remote areas not reached by the railroad. These were often boomtowns with a lot of bullion to guard and many people willing to steal it. (LoC)

and Billy Allen (a friend of the cowboys) backed this up, saying Holliday had fired first with his nickel-plated revolver. How or why he did this while holding a shotgun was not explained. Nevertheless, the sheriff's testimony turned much of the press against the Earp side.

Even more damning was the testimony of West Fuller, a neutral citizen who said Morgan and Doc fired the first shots and that Billy Clanton had his hands in the air. This was enough to get Wyatt Earp and Doc Holliday put in Behan's jail. Virgil and Morgan were still recovering from their wounds and were allowed to stay at home.

Riding to the rescue came an unlikely ally – Ike Clanton. When he took the stand he stuck to the story of the Earp party shooting first. Soon, however, his testimony about the gunfight and the hours leading up to it became entangled in contradictions and obvious falsehoods. He also told an elaborate tale of the Earps and Holliday being involved in the stagecoach attack that had left Philpot dead and claimed that they had gotten away with a large sum of money. Ike even claimed that they wanted to kill him since he knew too much. Of course, no money had been taken in that attack and Wyatt could have easily shot him while Ike was pleading for dear life at the O.K. Corral. Ike was such a terrible witness for the prosecution that he did more than the defense attorney in unraveling their case.

The case soon started to shift. Testimony from several eyewitnesses showed that Ike had been trying to start a fight for hours and had issued numerous threats. Sills and another neutral eyewitness said the cowboys had not had their hands in the air. Sills went on to say that after Virgil Earp had put his own hands in the air, Wyatt Earp and Billy Clanton had fired the first shots almost simultaneously. More damning evidence against the prosecution came from assistant district attorney Winfield Scott Williams, who testified that Behan said he had failed to disarm the cowboys, a direct contradiction to what the sheriff had told the Earp faction.

On November 30, Judge Spicer ruled in favor of the defense. He stated there was no evidence that the Earp faction planned to commit murder and that they had acted within the law in trying to disarm the cowboys. Whether or not Tom McLaury had a gun was immaterial since he was part of a group resisting arrest. The judge did, however, censure Virgil for bringing along men who had such bitter feuds with those he intended to disarm, considering it a bad judgment call that exacerbated the situation. He then tempered this criticism by admitting Virgil was in mortal danger and needed all the help he could get. The Earps and Holliday went free but their fight was only just beginning.

Nobody in Tombstone was fooled into thinking that legal vindication would let the Earps off the hook with the cowboys. Neither side was about to ride off into the sunset as the credits rolled. Both were established in the area, with property, business dealings, and family in the town and county. A bigger motive, pride, also kept the combatants from moving.

At first the war remained a war of words. It was as if the gunfight had shocked everyone into taking a step back. That did not mean, however, that anyone was backing down. Words had escalated into bloodshed before, and would again.

Tombstone proved to be a small town in many ways. The two rival papers, the *Epitaph* and the *Nugget*, had offices across the street from each other. Only a block away stood another pair of bad neighbors. The cowboys kept a room at the Grand. The shutters in their hotel room were always closed, except for one that had been removed, leaving just enough space for a watchful eye and a rifle barrel. Across the street stood the Cosmopolitan Hotel, where the Earps had moved their families for safety. Virgil remained a U.S. marshal, although with his leg wound he wasn't doing much, and Wyatt was still his deputy.

Mayor John Clum, editor of the *Epitaph* and longtime supporter of the Earps, grew nervous about the seething tension. He appealed to President Chester A. Arthur to repeal the Posse Comitatus Act so the U.S. Government could arm the local Citizens Safety Committee and use the Army to destroy the outlaws. The president asked Congress to modify the Act so the Army could assist against border raiders, but Congress was slow to act. This high-level political activity did little to assuage the problems at the local level. Clum recalled later:

> It was rumored about town that several residents of Tombstone had been "marked for death" by the rustler-clan, and I was assured that my name was written well up toward the head of their grim list, which besides myself included the Earp brothers, Doc Holliday, Judge Spicer, Tom Fitch, Marshall Williams and one or two others whose names I do not now recall. And in order that we might more fully realize the certainty of our fate, it was whispered that the Death List had been prepared with most spectacular and dramatic ceremonials enacted at midnight within the recesses of a deep canyon, during which the names of the elect had been written in blood drawn from the veins of a murderer.

NOVEMBER 30, 1881

Judge Spicer finds members of Earp party not guilty of murder

While this sounds like paranoid rumor-mongering, Clum's fears appear to have been justified by events on the night of December 14, when he boarded a stage to head East on business. As the stage passed through Malcolm's Station four miles outside town, a voice from the darkness cried, "Hold!"

Almost immediately after this order, several shots were fired. The driver was hit in the leg and one of the horses severely wounded. The team panicked and bolted ahead. Clum drew a pair of six-shooters and prepared for the worst. It took the driver half a mile to control the team. As soon as the stagecoach came to a halt, Clum dismounted. He feared the stagecoach could be a target farther down the road and decided to walk. Clum could have returned to Tombstone easily enough, but apparently worried there might be an ambush awaiting him there too, so he struck out for Benson, 25 miles away. After a time he was able to borrow a horse, send a message back to Tombstone that he was safe, and continue on his way to Benson.

While Clum felt sure the attack had been an attempted assassination – saying the lack of a shotgun messenger indicated to any bandits that there were no valuables on board, and that nighttime runs never carried money anyway – the *Nugget* mocked him for a coward. Former judge James Reilly even hinted the Earps were behind the attack, bringing up the old rumor that the brothers were stage robbers. The *Epitaph* blasted its rival, claiming it was supporting the criminal element. Even the papers in San Francisco, where many investors in the mines lived, dubbed the *Nugget* "the Cowboy Organ."

The war of words escalated. County Commissioner Milt Joyce taunted Virgil Earp on the night of December 16, saying he'd been expecting a

SHERMAN McMASTER

Born to a prosperous family in Illinois, Sherman McMaster (1853–92) moved West sometime in the 1870s. His movements during this decade are unclear but he apparently spent time in Dodge City, where he met Wyatt Earp and Doc Holliday. He was already gaining a reputation as a tough customer and reportedly killed a man over a gambling dispute there. The case was ruled self-defense.

By September of 1878 he was in Texas working for the Texas Rangers. It was here that he met Curley Bill Brocious. Despite being on opposite sides of the law, the two hit it off and there is a rumor that McMaster sprang Curley Bill from jail. Like many figures in the Old West, McMaster straddled the line between law and crime as it suited him.

McMaster left the Texas Rangers and moved to New Mexico, where he apparently joined the Dodge City Gang of Las Vegas, New Mexico, robbing stagecoaches and rustling cattle. The gang got its name because many of its members had earned their reputations in Dodge City and other Kansas cow towns. Later, McMaster moved to Tombstone and started running with the cowboys. At the same time, he may have been giving information to the Earp faction for reasons that are unclear. He was present when his friend Morgan Earp was murdered. If he wasn't fully on the side of the Earps before, he certainly was after that.

According to genealogical research, the correct spelling of his name is "McMaster", although most contemporary sources and later scholars spell it "McMasters." He was considered well educated and spoke fluent Spanish. After his time with the Vendetta Ride, McMaster slipped into obscurity. He died in Colorado in 1892.

holdup ever since the Earps and Holliday got out of jail. This earned Joyce a slap in the face and threats from some armed Earp followers. The next night Joyce confronted Wyatt and Virgil in the Alhambra Saloon. This time he was armed and made a show to fight. The three were separated before words could turn into bullets.

If the Earps thought moving out of their isolated dwellings and into a busy hotel would make them safer, they were mistaken. The cowboys' room at the Grand looked right on to the Earp quarters at the Cosmopolitan. Soon the Earps got a visit from Jack Altman, a clerk at the Grand, who warned them that various leaders among the cowboys such as Johnny Ringo, Curley Bill, Ike Clanton, and Pony Diehl had a room and were waiting for the right moment to strike.

On December 28, that moment came. At around 11:30pm, Virgil Earp stepped out of the Oriental Saloon to head back to his room. A moment later, three double-barreled shotguns fired on him from an unfinished building about 60ft away. Virgil fell with several pellets in his left arm and the left side of his body. Witnesses saw three figures hurry through the darkness, leaving the building and heading for a gulch on the edge of town.

DECEMBER 28, 1881

Virgil Earp wounded by three unknown gunmen

Diarist George Parsons was sitting in the Golden Eagle Brewery saloon nearby and nearly got hit by three pellets that shattered the window. He related in his journal, "Cries of 'There they go,' 'Head them off' were heard but the cowardly apathetic guardians of the peace were not inclined to risk themselves and the other brave men all more or less armed did nothing."

Virgil staggered back into the Oriental where Wyatt took him into his care and fetched two doctors. The diagnosis was grim. While the pellets had missed all the vital organs, Virgil's left humerus was shattered and the doctors debated whether the arm should be amputated. The marshal was teetering between life and death and the doctors were not sure he would make it. His wife Allie wept and was distraught, but the lawman tried to comfort her by saying, "Never mind, I've got one arm left to hug you with."

Wyatt soon named two of the killers. He said Virgil had spotted Stilwell entering the vacant building just as he (Virgil) was leaving the Oriental. Also, an examination of the building revealed Ike Clanton's hat, easily identified by the owner's name written on the inside.

Wyatt telegraphed U.S. Marshal Crawley Dake in Phoenix: "Virgil was shot by concealed assassins last night. His wounds are fatal. Telegraph me appointment with power to appoint deputies. Local authorities are doing nothing. The lives of other citizens are threatened." Dake wired back that same day giving Wyatt the authority to appoint deputies to assist him.

Wyatt did not strike back immediately. Instead he stayed close to Virgil's bedside. As Wyatt and the rest of his family watched Virgil struggle for life, another drama was being enacted on the streets of Tombstone. It was time for municipal elections, and the main issue was which side of the feud was right and which side was wrong. More than pride was at stake – holding the local offices gave access to a huge amount of revenue and patronage.

The *Epitaph* lambasted Behan and his cohorts as the "Ten Percent Ring," a group of corrupt officials who skimmed 10 percent off tax

Morgan Earp in a photograph taken *c.* 1881. Morgan was 30 years old in this picture and died the following year. (Arizona Historical Society, photo #29952)

revenues. "If the Ten-per-cent Ring get control of the city government as it already has that of the county," it editorialized, "there will be no other way for a man to live in this community except to join the ring or the rustlers."

The *Nugget* backed the People's Independent Party. One editorial read, "The election will to-day decide whether Tombstone is to be dominated for another year by the Earps and their strikers. Every vote against the People's Independent Ticket is a vote in favor of the Earps. Miners, business men and all others having the welfare of our city at heart should remember this."

The election on January 3, 1882, was a huge victory for the Behan–*Nugget* faction, with the vast majority of offices going to the People's Independent Party. For the Earps this was a stinging blow. Their attempts at bringing law and order as they saw it had been roundly rejected. They were vilified as vigilantes, not praised as lawmen, and their brand of peacekeeping was not welcome.

Just days after the election, Cochise County was again rocked with major crimes. On January 6 and 7, two stagecoaches were robbed. The first was a Tombstone stage headed to Bisbee with the miners' payroll in a Wells Fargo shipment. As the stagecoach passed along a road near the Clanton ranch, three men appeared and ordered it to stop. The stagecoach driver urged on the horses as the guard fired at the robbers. The bandits fired back, wounding one of the horses. This ended the fight and the bandits took their shipment. The *Los Angeles Times* fingered Ringo but did not reveal its source.

The second stagecoach did not have a shipment, so the bandits relieved the passengers of their cash. One of the passengers was Jim Hume, a Wells Fargo agent. This double humiliation did not sit well with Wells Fargo management.

Hume had not been sleeping on the job. Although the two masked bandits had the drop on him and he chose not to fight back since there was no shipment to protect, he did engage the robbers in conversation and took careful note of their physical characteristics and speech patterns. He was almost certain that he recognized them as two men who lived in the small settlement of Charleston, a cowboy haunt.

Hume asked Wyatt, Morgan, Wells Fargo spy Fred Dodge, and the Earps' friend Charlie Smith to go to the Charleston saloon of Jeptha Ayer, one of Dodge's informants. They found Hume already there, drinking with the suspects and playing dumb in the hope that they'd spill enough information to incriminate themselves. Whether they were wise to Hume's game or simply cautious is unclear, but they kept mum. Once again, criminals thwarted the law.

Again there were whisperings that the Earp faction was behind the robberies. The *Nugget*, which had recently run a story predicting (and hoping) the Earps would leave town, stated, "Who robbed the Bisbee stage? Six thousand dollars is a good stake to leave the country on, and we suggest they leave."

On January 17 came another flashpoint when Doc Holliday and Johnny Ringo nearly started a gunfight in the middle of the street. The various accounts of this encounter are so inflated and contradictory that it is impossible to say what actually took place. Ringo biographer Jack Burrows commented, "No near-gunfight in the history of the Old West (not a single shot was fired) has been burdened with so many grossly inaccurate and personally intrusive accounts." Whatever happened, the two went on their way unscathed.

With Virgil on the mend, Wyatt felt confident enough to strike back. He headed out of Tombstone with a posse including Morgan and Warren Earp, Holliday, Sherman McMaster, Turkey Creek Jack Johnson, Texas Jack Vermillion, Charlie Smith, and two others whose names have been lost. Each man was armed with a shotgun, a Winchester rifle (probably the carbine type favored on the range), two pistols, and 100 rounds. They carried warrants for brothers Ike and Fin Clanton as well as Pony Diehl.

The posse was supposed to have been funded by territorial marshal Crawley Dake, but it appears Dake kept most of the money for himself and Wyatt had to get the bulk of his men's funds from the law-and-order crowd in Tombstone. To complicate matters, another posse went chasing after Ringo, who had skipped his bond on two charges of robbery. Ringo returned to Tombstone and surrendered himself to Behan, a safer option than taking his chances with the posse. He claimed there had been a mix-up with the bond and that he thought he had been free to go. Earp's posse also came back empty-handed. They had entered Charleston with local cowboy Ben Maynard held in front of them at gunpoint as a precaution against ambush. Fortunately for Maynard, all the suspects had fled and he wasn't used as Wyatt's bulletproof vest. The posse scoured the countryside for days, as did a second posse that headed out on the same quest. Ike and Fin Clanton surrendered themselves to this posse on the condition that it would protect them from the Earp crowd.

The Earp posse came back to Tombstone under strange circumstances. City marshal and deputy sheriff Dave Neagle tracked the men down with a warrant for one of their number, Sherman McMaster. It turned out McMaster was wanted for horse theft, a charge Virgil Earp had tried and failed to bring him in for a while before. Perhaps McMaster felt that allying himself with the

Frontier justice. These five men were legally hanged on March 8, 1884 after killing several people during the robbery in Bisbee. The Goldwater and Castaneda store was the drop point for the Copper Queen Mine and the robbers thought that a $7,000 payroll was there. In fact it had not yet arrived. Enraged, the robbers went on a shooting spree and killed four people, including a pregnant woman. They were all hanged from one scaffold on the Cochise County courthouse yard. One of the men hanged on it, Dan Dowd, remarked that the multiple gallows looked like a "regular choking machine." (LoC)

Earps at this tough time would get him off the hook, but he was wrong. He gave himself up to Neagle and the rest of the Earp posse followed them back to Tombstone to ensure McMaster's safety.

McMaster was released on bail and for some reason his case never went to trial. The Clantons were in for a more serious time. They had been under the impression that they were being charged with one or more of the stagecoach robberies (perhaps because they were guilty?) but instead found themselves charged with the attempted murder of Virgil. Remarkably for such a serious charge, Judge William Stilwell (no relation to Frank Stilwell) set the bail at $1,500 each, which the suspects promptly paid.

The Earps received another blow. With Virgil temporarily unable to resume his duties, John Carr, the new mayor, named his replacement – none other than human shield Ben Maynard.

The next morning, February 2, Virgil and Wyatt formally resigned as deputy U.S. marshals. Their resignation letter reads in part:

> … there has arisen so much harsh criticism in relation to our operations, and such a persistent effort having been made to misrepresent and misinterpret our acts, we are led to the conclusion that, in order to convince the public that it is our sincere purpose to promote the public welfare, independent of any personal emolument or advantages to ourselves, it is our duty to place our resignations as deputy United States marshals in your hands …

Territorial Marshal Dake refused the resignation. To substitute for Virgil, he appointed John Henry Jackson, the leader of the other posse that had gone to find Ringo and the Clantons, as deputy marshal. This must have cheered Wyatt Earp, who was apparently weary of the feud. He even tried to patch things up with Ike Clanton. The *Nugget* reported in its February 2 issue that Wyatt "wished to interview with him with a view of reconciling their differences and obliterating the animosity that now exists between them. Mr. Clanton most emphatically declined to hold any communication whatever with Earp."

Ike must have felt he had the upper hand. Two days before, Pony Diehl and Fin Clanton had been found innocent of shooting Virgil, the judge citing lack of evidence. The same day the *Nugget* article appeared, Ike went into court. He claimed he had lost his hat some time before and didn't know how it had appeared at the scene of the shooting. While this weak excuse must have raised some eyebrows, the evidence was too circumstantial to convict, and he too was let off.

TURKEY CREEK JACK JOHNSON

Little is known for certain about "Turkey Creek" Jack Johnson (1852?–87?). His origins and even his real name are in question. Wyatt Earp believed he was a bookkeeper from Missouri named John Blunt or Blount who fled the state with his brothers after being involved in a gunfight. He may also have been a marshal in Nebraska. One story relates that he was in Deadwood, Dakota Territory, and had a fight with two men. He told them to meet him at the local graveyard to shoot it out. Johnson hired some gravediggers to dig two graves, then shot down his enemies when they showed up. He is also reputed to have spent time in Dodge City.

He could have met Wyatt Earp in either of these two places. Wyatt referred to him as an "old friend" by the time of the Tombstone incidents, although in another account Wyatt seems to indicate that he became familiar with him only after Johnson came to Tombstone. It appears Johnson arrived in Tombstone with the cowboys during an 1878 cattle drive with Sherman McMaster, Pony Diehl, and Curley Bill Brocious. Johnson continued working with the cowboys, going down to Mexico to rustle cattle. Wyatt claimed Johnson grew tired of that after a time and started acting as an informant for the Earp faction. The motivation for this change of heart is unclear, although some writers assert that he did it to persuade Wyatt and Wells Fargo to help him get his brother Bud out of jail.

Even Johnson's colorful nickname is in doubt. It first appears in Stuart Lake's blood-and-thunder biography of Wyatt Earp. Contemporary newspapers and Wyatt's own correspondence, however, never use this nickname. Lake may have simply added it to give some flair to an otherwise obscure figure.

After the Vendetta Ride, Johnson kept a low profile. Records from a Salt Lake City Masonic Lodge have him dying there in 1887, although it is not certain this is the same man.

Tombstone only had one lynching, that of John Heath on February 22, 1884. He was lynched after admitting in court that he had masterminded the Bisbee robbery that left four people dead. He had a long criminal record and his saloon in Bisbee was a well-known hangout for criminals. Heath insisted that the shooting was never part of the plan, and since he wasn't there, he was given life in prison instead of a death sentence. Enraged Bisbee citizens descended on Tombstone, dragged him out of jail, and strung him up. The coroner's inquest read, "We the undersigned, a jury of inquest, find that John Heath came to his death from emphysema of the lungs – a disease common in high altitudes – which might have been caused by strangulation, self-inflicted or otherwise." Heath was one of many Frontier men who walked on both sides of the law. He briefly served as deputy sheriff of Cochise County in the early 1880s. (LoC)

Wyatt was enraged. He later said that Judge Stilwell took him aside and said, "Wyatt, you'll never clean up this crowd this way; next time you'd better leave your prisoners out in the brush where alibis don't count."

So who did shoot Virgil Earp? It has been debated ever since. Cowboy Johnny Barnes later bragged to Fred Dodge that he and Pony Diehl did it. He made no mention of a third shooter.

Now that he was free, Ike Clanton decided to get revenge by bringing the Earps and Holliday up on murder charges for the O.K. Corral shootout. Behan threw them in jail, but unsurprisingly the judge let them go since they had already been found innocent of these charges and the plaintiff failed to offer any new evidence. Why Ike thought a second trial would come out any differently than the first is a mystery.

Another mystery came shortly after, when Wells Fargo agent Marshall Williams skipped town in the company of a prostitute, leaving a heap of debt. Fred Dodge would later say Williams was the cowboy mole inside the Wells Fargo company. Was Williams at fault for the stagecoach robberies, inadvertently staining the Earps' and Holliday's reputations? Those who held suspicions against the Earps would have pointed out that it was Williams who had hired Wyatt Earp as shotgun rider for Wells Fargo. It is just one more rumor and mystery in a town that made its reputation on rumors and mysteries.

For a time things quietened down. There were no major crimes and both factions lay low. This led Morgan Earp, always impulsive, to gain a false sense of security. On March 18, ignoring Wyatt's advice to stay out of sight, he went off to see the show *Stolen Kisses*. Afterwards he ran into Wyatt and asked him to play a game of pool. Although Wyatt had heard some vague warnings of trouble brewing, he went along against his better judgment.

With his back to a glass door, Morgan lined up a shot. Suddenly a bullet shattered the pane. Morgan slammed against the pool table, the slug passing right through him and wounding an innocent bystander. A second bullet lodged in the wall just above Wyatt's head. Two of Wyatt's friends ran into the alley but saw no one. Morgan lay in excruciating pain and lasted barely an hour. Wyatt stayed by his side and promised his brother he would hunt down and kill Morgan's murderers.

The Vendetta Ride

Wyatt Earp had had enough. He sat down to have a talk with Virgil. "Now, Virgil, I want you to go home," he later recalled saying. "I am going to try to get those men who killed Morgan, and I can't look after you and them too. So you go home." Wyatt gathered some friends and took Virgil and Allie to the train station at Contention. The couple would take Morgan's body to the family home at Colton, California, to be buried, and would stay there themselves for the foreseeable future.

Friends at Contention met them with some grim news. Cowboys Ike Clanton, Billy Miller, Frank Stilwell, and an unnamed fourth man were watching every train going through Tucson, which was on Virgil's route. Observers said they had spotted sawed-off shotguns tied under the

William S. Hart was one of the greatest cowboy stars of the silent screen, despite his never having worked as an actual cowboy. He befriended an aging Wyatt Earp and thrilled to his tales of real-life Western adventure. Hart encouraged Wyatt to set down his memoirs with the help of John Flood. The movie star did his best to get the manuscript accepted by publishers, but it never happened. Hart served as pallbearer at Wyatt's funeral. (LoC)

MARCH 18, 1882

Morgan Earp assassinated by unknown gunmen

cowboys' overcoats. Wyatt and Warren Earp, along with Holliday, Turkey Creek Jack Johnson, and Sherman McMaster decided to accompany Virgil through Tucson.

As they pulled into the city on March 20, they saw the cowboys fading into the crowd. Virgil's heavily armed escort helped him and Allie into a nearby hotel to dine and wait for the connecting train. Engineer S. A. Batman remembered the scene, recounting how he

> ... saw a man with a Winchester rifle walking up and down by the side of the train and was told that the man in question was one of the Earps guarding a party that were going through to California; shortly afterwards saw a man and lady come out of the hotel, the man carrying one arm in a sling; two men carrying Winchester rifles walked behind them. They got on the cars, the one outside still looking everywhere.

Opposite:
The route of the Earp posse's Vendetta Ride.

Virgil and Allie's guards escorted the couple to their seats and checked the carriages. As the train pulled out of Tucson, Virgil sat with his wife in the

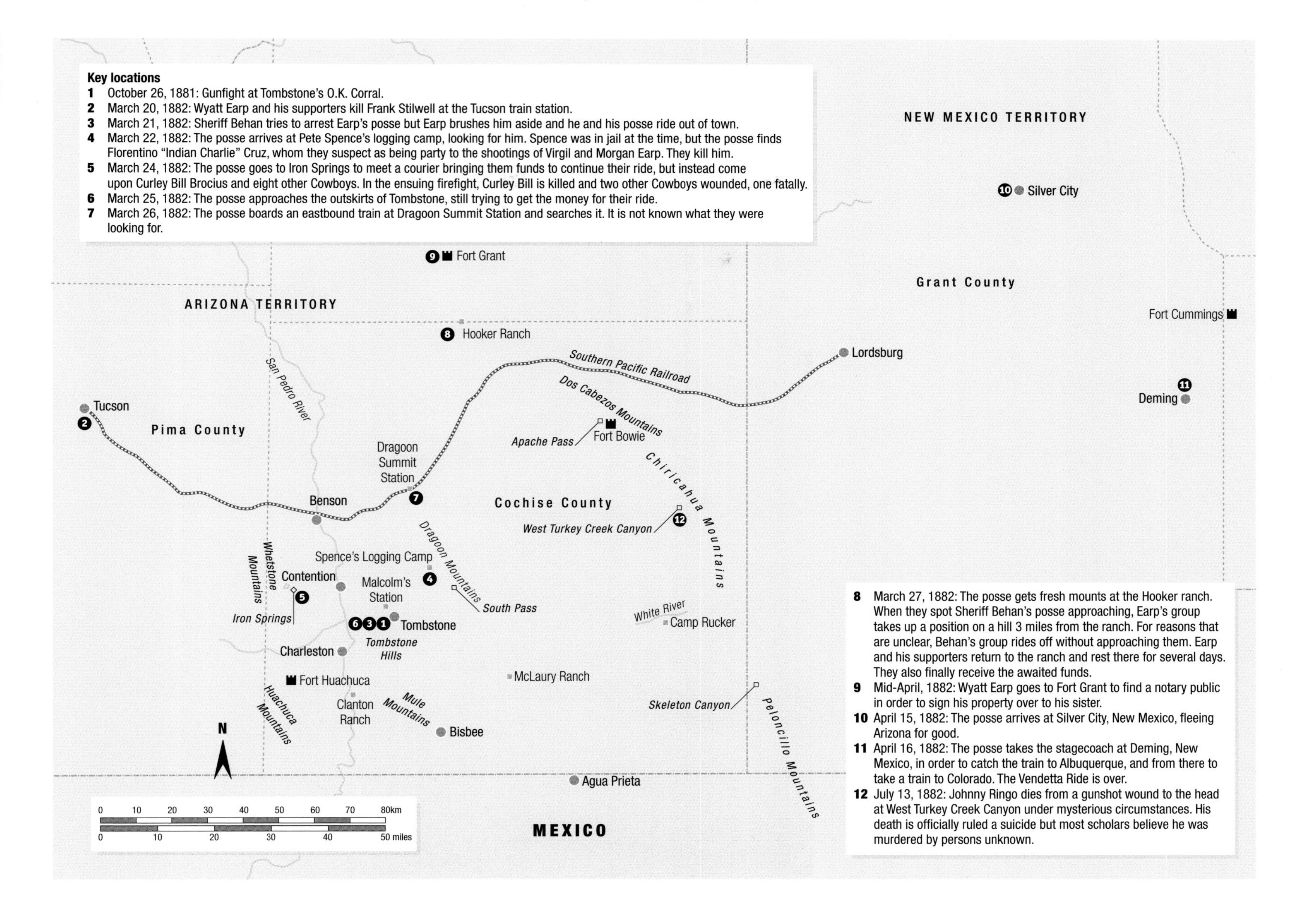

Key locations
1 October 26, 1881: Gunfight at Tombstone's O.K. Corral.
2 March 20, 1882: Wyatt Earp and his supporters kill Frank Stilwell at the Tucson train station.
3 March 21, 1882: Sheriff Behan tries to arrest Earp's posse but Earp brushes him aside and he and his posse ride out of town.
4 March 22, 1882: The posse arrives at Pete Spence's logging camp, looking for him. Spence was in jail at the time, but the posse finds Florentino "Indian Charlie" Cruz, whom they suspect as being party to the shootings of Virgil and Morgan Earp. They kill him.
5 March 24, 1882: The posse goes to Iron Springs to meet a courier bringing them funds to continue their ride, but instead come upon Curley Bill Brocius and eight other Cowboys. In the ensuing firefight, Curley Bill is killed and two other Cowboys wounded, one fatally.
6 March 25, 1882: The posse approaches the outskirts of Tombstone, still trying to get the money for their ride.
7 March 26, 1882: The posse boards an eastbound train at Dragoon Summit Station and searches it. It is not known what they were looking for.
8 March 27, 1882: The posse gets fresh mounts at the Hooker ranch. When they spot Sheriff Behan's posse approaching, Earp's group takes up a position on a hill 3 miles from the ranch. For reasons that are unclear, Behan's group rides off without approaching them. Earp and his supporters return to the ranch and rest there for several days. They also finally receive the awaited funds.
9 Mid-April, 1882: Wyatt Earp goes to Fort Grant to find a notary public in order to sign his property over to his sister.
10 April 15, 1882: The posse arrives at Silver City, New Mexico, fleeing Arizona for good.
11 April 16, 1882: The posse takes the stagecoach at Deming, New Mexico, in order to catch the train to Albuquerque, and from there to take a train to Colorado. The Vendetta Ride is over.
12 July 13, 1882: Johnny Ringo dies from a gunshot wound to the head at West Turkey Creek Canyon under mysterious circumstances. His death is officially ruled a suicide but most scholars believe he was murdered by persons unknown.
NEW MEXICO TERRITORY
ARIZONA TERRITORY
MEXICO
Pima County
Cochise County
Grant County
Silver City
Fort Grant
Fort Cummings
Hooker Ranch
Lordsburg
Deming
Tucson
Southern Pacific Railroad
Dos Cabezos Mountains
San Pedro River
Apache Pass
Fort Bowie
Dragoon Summit Station
Chiricahua Mountains
Benson
West Turkey Creek Canyon
Dragoon Mountains
Whetstone Mountains
Spence's Logging Camp
Contention
Malcolm's Station
Iron Springs
South Pass
Tombstone
White River
Camp Rucker
Tombstone Hills
Charleston
McLaury Ranch
Fort Huachuca
Mule Mountains
Clanton Ranch
Skeleton Canyon
Huachuca Mountains
Bisbee
Peloncillo Mountains
N
Agua Prieta
0 10 20 30 40 50 60 70 80km
0 10 20 30 40 50 miles

carriage, a pistol at the ready. Wyatt was prowling around outside and spotted Frank Stilwell and another man he thought he recognized as Ike Clanton lying on a flatcar in the darkness nearby, shotguns at the ready. Wyatt concluded they were about to snipe at his brother, who could clearly be seen through a lighted window.

As soon as they spotted Wyatt, the two gunmen fled. One was too slow, however. Wyatt recalled in a *Denver Republican* interview dated May 14, 1893:

> I ran straight for Stilwell. It was he who killed my brother. What a coward he was. He couldn't shoot when I came near him. He stood there helpless and trembling for his life. As I rushed upon him he put out his hands and clutched at my shotgun. I let go both barrels, and he tumbled down dead and mangled at my feet. I started for Clanton then, but he escaped behind a moving train of cars. When the train had passed I could not find him.

Virgil's train was now chugging out of the station. Wyatt ran up to his brother's window and mouthed the words "One for Morgan."

Wyatt's account makes it sound as if he faced off on Stilwell alone, but one witness said he saw four men chasing Stilwell. It seems Wyatt fired the fatal shot and his friends peppered the body with more bullets.

Artist's rendering, based upon a photograph, of Doc Holliday, *c.* 1880, when he was around 30 years old. He would grow thinner and age markedly in the final years before his death in 1887. (Arizona State Library, Archives and Public Records: History and Archives Division)

Ike Clanton, of course, told a tale slightly different than Wyatt's. Ike claimed he had heard that the Earp crew was coming to Tucson to kill him. He had accompanied Stilwell to the train station to meet a deputy from Charleston who was going to testify at his upcoming trial for the Bisbee stagecoach holdup. Ike recounted that he was waiting for Stilwell when Stilwell hurried up, hustled him out of sight, and told him that the Earps had arrived in Tucson on the train. Stilwell, according to Ike's version of events, didn't feel in danger and warned Ike to get out of town. Ike headed for his hotel and heard the shots shortly thereafter.

Several witnesses saw the killing, and a couple testified that the men cheered after gunning Stilwell down. When Stilwell's body was found the next morning it was found riddled with bullets and buckshot. Pellets from at least one shotgun blast had mangled his lower body, and another blast had hit his left leg. A bullet had passed from one side of his body to the other, puncturing both lungs. He also had bullet wounds in his right leg and left arm. One hand was severely burned by gunpowder, as if he had put it out to ward off death. Although a pistol was found on Stilwell's body, he hadn't drawn or fired it. Stilwell's corpse made a gruesome sight, with one witness saying he was the "worst shot-up man I ever saw."

It seems strange that Stilwell could be shot and left to lie for an entire night next to a busy depot. Perhaps people were scared away. The Tucson *Star* reported: "Several railroad hands, just after the shooting, chanced to approach going to their duties, and were warned back by the crowd of shooters." Big-Nose Kate later told the tale that everyone thought the shooting was in celebration of the lighting of gas lamps in Tucson for the first time that evening.

While the O.K. Corral gunfight wore a thin mantle of official authority, Stilwell's shooting was simply the killing of a man who had never been convicted of a crime. Most papers railed against Wyatt, the *Arizona Star* saying:

> ... without any provocation a band of four or five slayers pursued a lonely man in the dark and without a word of warning murdered him in cold blood and then hied to their stamping grounds as unconcerned as though they had been out on a hunting expedition, or like so many blood-thirsty Apaches rejoice over their crime.

More stunning news hit the papers. At the coroner's inquest for Morgan Earp, Pete Spence's wife Marietta said she was sure he had killed Morgan. Pete and his friends Indian Charlie (possibly Florentino Cruz), Frank Stilwell, "Freeze" (an alias for Frederick Bode), and a fifth man she didn't know had been going about armed and came back shortly after the shooting in a state of excitement. Pete Spence turned himself in to Behan's jail, and was allowed to keep a gun in case the Earps came seeking vengeance. When the case went to trial on April 2 it was thrown out because by law a wife could not testify against her husband.

After the Stilwell killing, Wyatt and his friends returned to Tombstone. Authorities in Tucson telegraphed Tombstone on March 21 to request that Behan arrest them on a charge of murder. The telegraph operator in Tombstone was a friend of the Earps and showed the message to them, saying he'd hold it for some time to give them a chance to skip town.

Behan got the message at about 8pm and hurried over to the Cosmopolitan to find the Earp party just leaving. They were all heavily armed. The *Nugget* reported they drew their guns on Behan, grabbed their horses, and galloped out of town. The *Epitaph* reported that while they were armed, they didn't point their weapons at the sheriff and merely brushed him off. Either way, Behan was wise not to try to stop them. Wyatt and his friends had vengeance on their minds and the rule of law no longer mattered to them.

Shortly thereafter, the last Earp family members in Tombstone, Wyatt's wife Mattie and Jim's wife Bessie, left for the safety of the family home in Colton. Records are unclear, but it appears Jim may have already left, keeping watch with a gun in hand on the train that carried Virgil and Allie to safety. Wyatt could now go on his vendetta without having to worry about his loved ones.

Wyatt Earp rode out of town with a tough group of men. Warren Earp was good with a gun, as was Doc Holliday. Texas Jack Vermillion may have been the best shot of them all. Sherman McMaster and Turkey Creek Jack Johnson had both rustled cattle with the cowboys but had also served as

Tombstone c. 1890. By this time the city had reached its largest extent and was in fact beginning its decline. The mines flooded and the silver was beginning to play out. (Arizona State Library, Archives and Public Records: History and Archives Division)

MARCH 20, 1882

Wyatt Earp and friends kill Frank Stilwell

Wyatt's informants. They'd run with a tough crowd and risked their lives for Wyatt, so he knew that he could rely on them. Charlie Smith either rode out of town with them, as the *Epitaph* reports, or may have gone ahead with a wagon, according to other narratives.

Behan was not about to let them go so easily. He rounded up a posse of a dozen men, including Johnny Ringo, Ike and Fin Clanton, and other cowboys, swore them in as deputies, and headed out.

MARCH 22, 1882

Wyatt Earp and his men kill Florentino Cruz at Pete Spence's logging camp

On March 22, Earp and his friends arrived at Pete Spence's logging camp at the South Pass of the Dragoon Mountains. This camp was a popular meeting spot for the cowboys, who used its relative isolation as a convenient place to rest up and change the brands on stolen cattle. Earp stopped a group of workers and asked them where Pete was. They told him he wasn't around; in fact he was still in Behan's jail under protective custody. As Earp and his group turned on to the road to Tombstone, they spotted Indian Charlie, whom Pete Spence's wife Marietta had said was involved in Morgan's murder. Another Mexican laborer, Simon Acosta, watched the action: "I immediately ran up the hill and saw them shooting at Florentino." Acosta went on:

> I did not see Florentino fall; I saw them following up the hill and firing at him. I did not pay attention to the number of shots fired. They stayed on top of the hill awhile, dismounted, and soon after went off ... When I saw Florentino, he was running away. The pursuing party spread out, some on each side, and others immediately following.

When Florentino's body was recovered it had four bullets in it. One had punctured the right temple and entered the brain, while another had entered the right side of the body and exited near the spine. The doctor who examined Florentino's corpse declared either of these "sufficient to cause death." In addition, Florentino had a bullet hole through his left thigh and a flesh wound on the right shoulder.

Wyatt later claimed that before they killed Florentino, the man confessed to Morgan's killing. We only have Wyatt's word for this, along with a probably false tale that he challenged Florentino to a shootout. There was no evidence the Mexican was even armed. Most newspapers reacted to this killing even more angrily than that of Stilwell's. At least Stilwell had had a gun; this new death was murder plain and simple. Researchers are also divided over whether Florentino Cruz really was Indian Charlie, since there are records of an Indian Charlie being brought in to share the jail with Pete Spence. Cruz may have been the unnamed extra gunman that Marietta Spence had seen, or perhaps a complete innocent. As with many aspects of the Earp Vendetta tale, the truth appears to be hopelessly obscured behind controversy, sparse records, and Frontier tale-telling.

While some newspapers vilified Earp and his men, others idealized Wyatt as an honorable man seeking vengeance. This idea got a boost from the executives of Wells Fargo, who in an interview with the San Francisco *Examiner* gave the rogue lawman their complete support and dismissed rumors of his involvement in the robbing of their stages. They explained that Wyatt could not surrender to Sheriff Behan because the sheriff would allow the cowboys to kill him. They even took a swipe at the ever-critical *Nugget*, calling it the "Cowboy Organ." Wyatt Earp was rising from being a local figure to the status of a Wild West legend.

MARCH 23, 1882

Charlie Smith and Dan Tipton enter Tombstone and are arrested

Shootout at Iron Springs

That legend now had two posses after him – Behan's and another made up of cowboys from Charleston led by Curley Bill. They claimed Behan had deputized them, although the sheriff later denied that. Such a trivial matter of law did not really matter at this point anyway.

Two longtime supporters and members of Wyatt's Vendetta Ride were already out of the picture. On March 23, Charlie Smith and Dan Tipton, who may have been present at the Florentino Cruz shooting, tried to sneak back into Tombstone. They were spotted and Behan arrested them for resisting arrest when they had left town with the Earp group on March 21. He also charged them with stopping an officer from fulfilling his duties – arresting the Earps for murdering Stilwell – through the use of threats, intimidation, firearms, and force.

Wyatt's group needed more money to continue the ride, so Wyatt sent word to friends in Tombstone to bring $1,000 to Iron Springs, now called Mescal Springs, in the Whetstone Mountains. The posse rode to the meeting point under a hot sun on March 24. As they descended a sloping trail and first spotted the muddy little spring, Wyatt got the feeling something was wrong. Here is a description of the scene based on Wyatt Earp's personal testimony as later told to (and elaborated by) his biographer Stuart Lake:

> The fork to Iron Springs climbed a narrow, rocky canon into the Whetstones, a veritable inferno beneath the desert sun, and, after two or three miles in which no sign appeared that others recently had used the trail, vigilance relaxed. Wyatt loosened the gun belts around his waist. Horses and men were weary and hot.
>
> About one hundred yards from the waterhole, the trail rounded a rocky shoulder and cut across a flat shelf of deep sand. Ahead, Iron Springs was hidden by an eroded bank possibly fifteen feet high. Beyond the hollow, where the mountain slope resumed, was a grove of cottonwoods. Between this grove and the waterhole was an abandoned shack, hidden from view by a bluff. Across the sandy stretch Wyatt rode, coat unbuttoned, six-guns sagging low, Winchester in the saddle boot, Wells Fargo shotgun

> and ammunition belt looped to the saddle horn. His horse had quickened at the scent of water and Wyatt let him make the gait.

An instant later, nine cowboys sprang up from the thicket of cottonwoods near the bank and began firing. Curley Bill was in the forefront with a shotgun in his hands. Texas Jack Vermillion's horse screamed and fell with a bullet in its body; Vermillion lay pinned and helpless underneath. Wyatt Earp leapt out of the saddle and leveled his shotgun while keeping the bridle over his arm. To his dismay he saw his companions

MARCH 24, 1882

Gunfight at Iron Springs

> disappearing in a cloud of dust as fast as their horses could carry them. My horse reared and tugged at the bridle in such a wild fashion that I could not regain the saddle. I reckoned that my time had come. But if I was to die, I proposed that Curley Bill at least should die with me.

Curley Bill had similar sentiments towards Wyatt Earp. The cowboy fired his shotgun and pellets tore through the edges of Earp's long coat, which were flapping open. Keeping his cool, Earp aimed his shotgun and gave Curley Bill both barrels in the chest. In a spurt of gore, Curley Bill fell half in the water and lay still.

The death of their leader did not stop the cowboys. They kept up a furious fusillade. Wyatt tried to grab his Winchester from its saddle sheath but, in a curious parallel with Tom McLaury's plight at the O.K. Corral, he couldn't control his horse enough to get it. Giving up, Wyatt went for his pistol and

TEXAS JACK VERMILLION

Although he worked at the uninspiring job of a carpenter, John Wilson "Texas Jack" Vermillion (1842–1911) was one of the flashier members of the Earp party. He wore his hair long down his back and everyone considered him an expert marksman and fearless in combat. When asked why he had the nickname "Texas Jack" despite having never lived in Texas, he replied, "Because I'm from Virginia." He later earned the nickname "Shoot-Your-Eye-Out" Vermillion. There is no record of anyone having the guts to ask him about that one.

Vermillion was born in Virginia and served in the Confederate Army during the Civil War. After the war he married, had two children, and moved to Missouri. Sadly, all three family members died in a diphtheria epidemic. This may have caused Vermillion to drift West and into history. He ended up in Dodge City, where he probably met the Earps and Holliday. His movements are unclear, but someone named Texas Jack killed a man near Flagstaff in 1881. Later that year Vermillion moved to Tombstone. Vermillion's first recorded contact with the Earps was when he worked for Virgil as a special deputy on June 22, 1881, protecting Tombstone from looters after a major fire. Some accounts state that he didn't know the Earps well but was close friends with Holliday and joined the Vendetta Ride out of loyalty to him.

Vermillion ended up back in Dodge City by 1883, where he shot and killed a man for cheating at cards. Later he moved in Denver, where he became part of the confidence racket run by the famous Colorado swindler Soapy Smith. In 1890 he returned to Virginia, remarried, and settled down to a quiet life. He died in 1911.

New research indicates that Texas Jack's real name may not have been John Wilson Vermillion, but rather John Oberland Vermillion, and in fact these were two different people.

Like his friend Wyatt Earp, John Clum couldn't settle down. In later life he left Tombstone and ended up as a U.S. postal inspector in the Alaska Territory during the 1898 Gold Rush and the later, more tranquil settlement period. He is shown here, mounted, making his rounds. (LoC)

discovered to his horror that the cartridge belt had fallen around his thighs and the guns had slipped to the back. Under constant fire he managed to pull one out and return fire. Cowboy Johnny Barnes went down, fatally wounded. Wyatt then tried to mount and make his getaway. Again his cartridge belt impeded him. Slung as low as it was, he couldn't spread his legs enough to get astride the saddle. He ended up lying on the horse's back trying to pull his belt up with one hand and holding onto the saddle horn with the other as bullets whizzed about him. A bullet struck the saddle horn, right between his nose and hand. The impact almost made him fall off but didn't otherwise hurt him. Another bullet clipped the heel of his boot.

Wyatt finally managed to fix his wardrobe malfunction and rode over to save Texas Jack Vermillion, who had finally gotten out from under his horse. Once his friend was safely up behind him, he galloped off to where his friends were waiting. Wyatt recalled, "When I got to the ground, I found that the skirts of my coat, which had been held out at my sides by my leather holsters, had been riddled to shreds." His friends were amazed to find Wyatt unhurt. Wyatt felt the same. The impact on his heel had numbed his leg and he felt sure he'd been shot there. Holliday proposed another charge, but Wyatt felt they had been lucky enough for one day and ordered a retreat.

The couriers who had their money arrived at the battle scene shortly afterwards, only to find the angry cowboys and a dead body. They wisely pretended they were chasing some lost mules and were invited to share a meal with the cowboys, who treated them to the story of the gunfight. The couriers then made their excuses and hurried back to Tombstone. The "Battle of Iron Springs," as it was heralded in the headlines, made national news. Wyatt Earp's reputation, controversial as it was, had been firmly made.

The cowboys buried Curley Bill in an unknown location and split up. One group saw no reason why the death of one of their leaders should interfere with business and promptly stole four mules from a Mexican and $200 from a pair of Chinese restaurant owners. Not content with the money, they also took the Chinese men's clothes and fired at them as they fled naked through the desert.

Several tales have grown up about the gunfight at Iron Springs. The most intriguing is that Curley Bill was not killed. The *Nugget* offered $1,000 for proof of his death, and the *Epitaph* offered $2,000 donated to charity if Curley Bill showed up at their offices. Both prizes went unclaimed. There were sightings of him across the country and a few old-timers spun tales of seeing him years after his supposed death. While these stories make for good reading, it is likely that Curley Bill did actually die at Iron Springs. The Wild West abounds in legends of heroes and villains living past their supposed date of death. Jesse James, Billy the Kid, and many others all had these stories grow up around them. There were even imposters, usually old-timers from the West who knew enough about life back then to spin a convincing tale to a gullible public.

Wyatt's posse, if it could be called such at this point, returned to the outskirts of Tombstone to find out what was happening. By this time Dan Tipton and Charlie Smith were free. Their attorney pointed out that they couldn't have resisted arrest because Behan did not, in fact, have a warrant in his hand. Charlie Smith slipped out of town to join the posse on March 25. They then left the Tombstone area and rode to the Dragoon Mountains,

The battle of Iron Springs (overleaf)

On March 24, 1882, Wyatt Earp and his companions rode to Iron Springs, about 20 miles west of Tombstone. They were to meet a friend to collect $1,000 to pay expenses for their continued Vendetta Ride. It was a hot day and the group was spread out, with Wyatt Earp and Texas Jack Vermillion riding in front and the others lagging behind. Wyatt's hot and heavy cartridge belt was bothering him, so he loosened it. They climbed a narrow, rocky canyon along a trail that appeared not to have been used for some time.

As they rounded a rocky shoulder they saw a long stretch of exposed sand. The spring was out of sight down a wash perhaps 15ft down. As Wyatt and Texas Jack crested the bluff they saw nine cowboys by the spring cooking a meal. They were Curley Bill, Charles "Pony" Diehl, Johnny Barnes, Ed and Johnny Lyle, Milt and Bill Hicks, Rattlesnake Bill Johnson, and Frank Patterson.

The cowboys fired first, hitting Texas Jack's horse. The horse reared and fell over, dead. Texas Jack was pinned and helpless underneath it. Wyatt jumped off his horse and, holding the reins in his left hand, grabbed his double-barreled shotgun with his right. The rest of his followers galloped away, thinking the front two would follow.

Curley Bill blasted at Wyatt with his shotgun and tore the tails of Wyatt's long coat but did not hit him. Wyatt leveled his shotgun and gave Curley Bill both barrels in the stomach. He tossed the smoking shotgun aside and tried to grab his Winchester from its saddle sheath, but his horse panicked from the gunfire and the sight of its dead companion.

After a moment's struggle Wyatt gave up. He went for his pistols, only to find his cartridge belt had slipped down to his thighs. As bullets zinged all around him, he went through several contortions to grab a pistol and draw it. Now he was on familiar ground again and put a bullet into Johnny Barnes, fatally wounding him. He also wounded Milt Hicks in the arm.

The odds were now six-to-one, better but still discouraging. Knowing he couldn't survive for long, Wyatt tried to mount, only to find he couldn't get his legs open enough to sit astride. The cartridge belt was like a rope tied around him. Wyatt ended up lying flat on the bucking horse's back, trying to dodge bullets, hang on, and pull up his belt all at the same time. Somehow he managed to do all three. By then Texas Jack had extricated himself and jumped up behind him. Together they galloped to their friends and safety.

Wyatt and his posse held a brief council of war and decided against a charge. They hurried away to fight another day.

where at 1pm on March 26 they boarded an eastbound train stopped at Dragoon Summit Station to check the cars, apparently looking for someone among the passengers.

On March 27 they holed up at the ranch of Henry Clay Hooker, one of the most prominent ranchers in the region. While the cowboys spared small ranchers, and in fact used them as willing or unwilling hosts while on the job, they considered big ranches to be fair game. Hooker had lost numerous cattle to the rustlers and along with other members of the Cattlegrowers Association had offered a $1,000 reward for the death of Curley Bill. Hooker later said he offered Wyatt the reward and Wyatt replied, "I don't want any reward for carrying out my promise to Morgan. If the Cattlegrowers Association feel they owe me anything, let them pay you for the horses you have given us."

A side drama played out near Tombstone as the posse rested itself and its horses at the Hooker ranch. Deputy Sheriff Breakenridge, the law in town while Behan scoured the countryside for the Earp faction, set out to a ranch eight miles outside Tombstone to arrest a pair of cowboys on several charges. The cowboys fought back, with one deputy killed and two wounded. The two cowboys were also wounded before they could be disarmed and arrested. One of the outlaws died of his wounds, while the other discovered that his hospital room was unguarded and managed to walk away. As usual, law enforcement was uneven when it came to the cowboys.

Wyatt's rest at the Hooker ranch was soon interrupted by the approach of several horsemen. He assumed it was one of the posses gunning for them and so he and his friends saddled up and lit out for a bluff three miles away. This would give them advantageous ground. Wyatt was correct: it was the posse led by Sheriff Behan. One of Hooker's ranch hands reported to the *Epitaph* that:

> Sheriff Behan asked Mr Hooker if he knew the whereabouts of the Earp party. Mr Hooker replied that he did not know and if he did he would not tell him. Sheriff Behan then said, "You must be upholding murderers and outlaws then."
> "No sir, I am not. I know the Earps and I know you and I know they have always treated me like gentlemen; damn such laws and damn you and damn your posse. They are a set of horse thieves and outlaws."

One of the posse members snapped, "Damn the son of a bitch, he knows where they are and let us make him tell."

At this point Hooker's foreman came forward with a Winchester at the ready and said, "You can't come here into a gentleman's yard and call him a son of a bitch. Now you skin it back. Skin it back. If you are looking for a fight and come here to talk that way, you can get it before you find the Earps. You can get it right here."

After a bit more back and forth things cooled down enough for the posse to be given breakfast. The code of hospitality on the Frontier was a hard thing to break. Behan then rode to Fort Grant to try and get some Apache scouts. According to Hooker, Colonel James Biddle refused to give him any, although Behan claims they had been let go and were no longer at the fort. The Earps returned to the Hooker ranch and got a shipment of $2,000 to meet expenses; half was the money that they had tried to pick up at Iron Springs and the other half came from Wells Fargo.

For a time details of the group's movements became sketchy. The men may have spent the following days holed up at the Hooker ranch. There were vague rumors of more gunfights, but it is unclear if they were real battles or idle talk. They showed up at Silver City, New Mexico, on April 15, where they sold their horses and took a stagecoach to Fort Cummings, 20 miles northeast of Deming. From there they took a train to Albuquerque. After staying in that city for about a week, they took a train to Colorado. The Vendetta Ride was over.

Or was it? There remained two final, strange chapters to the tale. The first came when Doc Holliday was arrested in Denver on May 15 for the murder of Frank Stilwell. He and Wyatt had parted ways over some argument that remains obscure and now Doc had gone to Denver with Bat Masterson while Wyatt remained in Trinidad, Colorado. Doc was walking along one night when a man appeared out of the shadows with a pair of six-shooters leveled at him. He identified himself as an Arizona lawman named Perry Mallen and took Doc to the sheriff's office, where he charged him with the murders of Stilwell, Curley Bill, Billy Clanton, two more men, and several lesser crimes. Doc told the sheriff that Mallen was a fraud. This soon became apparent as Mallen kept changing his story. It was obvious that Holliday knew the lawman, but wouldn't reveal who "Mallen" really was. Meanwhile Bat Masterson came to Holliday's rescue by trumping up a bogus minor charge in Colorado to keep him from being extradited to Arizona. Holliday was cleared of the Colorado charge, of course, and was soon free to roam the saloons and gambling houses again.

Stranger events were going on in Arizona. On July 14, Johnny Ringo was found dead near a stream in West Turkey Creek Canyon in the Chiricahua Mountains. He had a gunshot wound to the head and a gun in his hand. There were some strange elements to the scene. A small part of Ringo's scalp had been cut away. His horse was missing and was found later with Ringo's boots slung over the saddle. Ringo himself was wearing a ripped-up shirt wrapped around his feet, but the condition of these makeshift moccasins showed that he hadn't walked far in them. Also, Ringo's cartridge belt was on upside down.

The death was ruled a suicide, a verdict supported both by Ringo's biographer and by many people who knew the cowboy, who was well known for his fits of depression and frequent allusions to suicide. There are persistent tales, however, of one of the members of the Vendetta Ride, probably Wyatt Earp, slipping back into Arizona to get rid of this prominent enemy who, the Tucson *Star* said, "was known in this section as 'King of the Cowboys.'" In later years Wyatt did claim to have killed Ringo. An examination of Wyatt's known movements, however, makes it unlikely that he could have left Colorado, hunted down and shot Ringo, and returned. This last gunshot remains another mystery in the lore of the Old West.

AFTERMATH

Most of the major players in the drama of the Arizona War didn't live long. In Colorado Doc Holliday went into a steady decline, still gambling, drinking, and fighting until the tuberculosis that had plagued him for so long finally took his life on November 8, 1887. Billy Claiborne was killed by gambler/gunslinger "Buckskin Frank" Leslie in a gunfight at the Oriental on November 14, 1882. Ike and Fin Clanton were caught in the act of rustling cattle near Fort Grant in June of 1887. Ike was shot and killed when he didn't obey an order to halt. Fin ended up in a prison called the Yuma Hell Hole.

The Earps fared better. Despite his crippled arm, Virgil Earp went back to work as a lawman. He served as the first elected city marshal of Colton, California. He became restless, however, and hopped around various towns running saloons and speculating in mines before settling down once again as deputy sheriff of Goldfield, Nevada, where he died on October 19, 1905.

Wyatt Earp also felt restless. He had never sought fame; he came to the Frontier to find fortune. He got exactly the opposite of what he wanted. After he left the Arizona War behind him he was plagued by newspaper reports that periodically resurrected the old fight, adding garishly exaggerated details or complete fabrications. More often than not, Wyatt and his brothers came off as the bad guys. Even the old tale of their supposed stagecoach robbery was repeated as if it were fact.

Wyatt and Josie "Sadie" Marcus stayed in Colorado for a time, drifting around the various mining camps before ending up in San Diego, California, where Wyatt ran a saloon and made a name for himself racing horses. He followed gold strikes in Alaska and Nevada. While the years were catching up with him, he still didn't abandon his dreams of striking the mother lode. Wyatt and Josie settled in Los Angeles, where they met many early Western movie stars, and spent winters mining out in the California desert. He died on January 13, 1929.

THE LONG SHADOW OF THE CIVIL WAR

In the 1880s, the United States was still feeling the effects of the Civil War. Reconstruction had ended only a few years before and countless people still suffered from war wounds and grief for lost loved ones. In the South, many families never recovered economically and bitterness still ran high. Many of the principal and peripheral players in the Tombstone drama were involved in the Civil War. James, Virgil, and Newton Earp all fought in Illinois Union regiments.

James "Jim" Earp joined the 17th Illinois Infantry soon after the start of hostilities. Missouri, just to the south, looked like it might secede and the 17th Illinois was one of the many regiments from surrounding states sent in to keep it in the Union. On October 21, 1861, Jim's regiment saw action at the battle of Fredericktown in southeast Missouri. The Illinois troops were the key to victory, being in the thick of the fighting and suffering numerous casualties. Jim took a bullet in the shoulder that crippled his arm for life. He was invalided out and after the war joined his brothers in Tombstone. His infirmity kept him from joining in the gunfight at the O.K. Corral or the ensuing Vendetta Ride.

Virgil Earp joined the 83rd Illinois Infantry in July of 1862 and served until the end of the war. He seems to have been a lackluster soldier as he was never promoted and indeed was brought before a court martial. His offense is unknown, but it must have been minor since he was only docked two weeks' pay.

Although Doc Holliday was only a child during the Civil War, coming from a wealthy Georgia family he certainly felt its effects. The Hollidays were uprooted by the war and lost a considerable amount of money. In 1868, a teenaged Holliday and his friends decided to strike a blow against Reconstruction by planting a barrel of gunpowder under the Valdosta Courthouse (which also acted as the Freedman's Bureau) in Georgia during a speech by a Republican candidate for Congress. The youths were caught before they could go through with their plan. Because of his youth, Holliday appears not to have been punished. As an adult Doc apparently got over his resentment, since he threw in his lot with the Unionist Earps.

In the early years of the war, future sheriff Johnny Behan was living in San Francisco. He signed on as a civilian employee for Carleton's Column of Union Volunteers, the famous "California Column," which marched into New Mexico and Arizona to secure it for the Union. They met little resistance from the Confederates, who were already retreating, but had considerable trouble with the Apaches. At Apache Pass in southeast Arizona, an advance detachment of the California Column was ambushed by a superior force of Apaches on July 14–15, 1862. Behan, although only a civilian, fought alongside the troops. The Apaches were driven off and Fort Bowie was established to protect the pass and its water supply.

Ben Goodrich was the most prominent lawyer on the prosecution team at the Earps' and Holliday's murder trial. Hired by the cowboys, he was a Texan and a former lieutenant in a Confederate Texas regiment. Texas Jack Vermillion also fought for the Confederacy. Territorial Marshal Crawley Dake was a veteran of the Union Army who had been wounded in action. A marginal member of the Vendetta Ride, Dan Tipton, had served in the Union Navy.

More important than the service records of various individuals was the lingering rift in American politics. Tombstone had a chapter of the Grand Army of the Republic, an organization for Union veterans that, like all such societies at the time, also was a way to make business connections. Tombstone's business elite, as well as many of its regular citizens, came from the North and supported pro-business Republican policies. Many of the prospectors and ranchers came from the South, especially Texas, and thus had more Southern views. They hated the Republican Party for crushing the rebellion and voted Democrat.

The Democratic *Nugget*, with undersheriff Harry Woods as its editor, was eager to please out-of-town investors who read its weekly edition, and so it downplayed the crimes of the cowboys, while the Republican *Epitaph* tended to highlight them. Naturally the *Nugget* supported Behan and his political faction while the *Epitaph* supported the Earps.

Wyatt's jilted former wife Mattie went into a quick spiral of decline as a drug-addicted prostitute in the mining town of Pinal, Arizona, where she killed herself on July 3, 1888. Her treatment at the hands of her husband forever tarnishes Wyatt Earp's image of a just and noble lawman. Despite this, recent films and the tourist board of Tombstone have rehabilitated Earp's reputation. He has now come full circle, from flawed seeker of justice to larger-than-life badman to larger-than-life seeker of justice.

Surviving them all was Big-Nose Kate, the drunken, loud-mouthed prostitute who continued being a drunken, loud-mouthed prostitute for many years before settling down to the more sedate profession of running a (respectable) lodging house. She retired to the Arizona Pioneers Home and died on November 2, 1940, long after the events she had witnessed had passed into legend.

A miner and his ore cart near Prescott, Arizona Territory, *c.* 1898. While the saloons, gunfights, and women of easy virtue get the most attention, life in Old West mining towns was mostly dirty, backbreaking work. (Arizona State Library, Archives and Public Records: History and Archives Division)

CONCLUSION

The Arizona War brings up a fundamental question of justice: can a man take the law into his own hands when the police and courts fail to protect him? As far as Wyatt Earp and his friends were concerned, the answer was "yes." No court would convict the cowboys, who killed and stole with impunity. The Earps and their faction felt they had been hemmed into a corner and had no choice but to fight back.

But how effective was their response? Did the gunfight at the O.K. Corral and the ensuing Vengeance Ride break the power of the cowboys? By mid-1882, rustling and stagecoach robbing were indeed on the wane in southern Arizona, but it is debatable whether the Earps are to thank for this. Increased patrols by the Mexican army and increased vigilance by ranchers on both sides of the border may be the main reason that the rustlers looked for other work. Southern Arizona was also becoming more populated. Law tightened its grip on the land and the rowdy prospectors and cowboys were being outnumbered by an increasing number of shopkeepers and respectable laborers.

President Chester A. Arthur finally responded to the troubles in southeastern Arizona. His move to get the Posse Comitatus Act amended so the Army could go after outlaws got quashed in the Senate, so on May 3, 1882, he used his presidential authority to threaten the region with martial law if the outlaws didn't disperse and take up legal pursuits. But the worst of the violence had already ended. On May 21, the Tucson *Citizen* asserted that "Outlaws remain but are quiet and crime which has run riot in Cochise County for two years has made way for peace and quiet."

There is also the question of how much vengeance the Vendetta Ride actually accomplished. Ike and Fin Clanton were both very much alive. Johnny Ringo may have died at his own hand. Also, there were numerous other lesser cowboys who made it through unscathed. The reasons for this failure seem to have been lack of planning and willpower. The Earps were reacting to events rather than following a coherent strategy. The Earp faction did not plan and fight a war of annihilation against the cowboys. Instead they hit targets of opportunity and then fled the Arizona Territory when the legal situation became too hot for them. It appears that Wyatt and his friends were satisfied with simply getting rid of a few of their enemies in a tit-for-tat killing. Wyatt did not even eliminate all the main suspects in his brother Morgan's murder. Ike Clanton, the instigator of the gunfight at the O.K. Corral and an obvious suspect in the shooting of Virgil, was allowed to go free.

Why did the Earp faction stop when it did? This is yet another of the enduring mysteries of this strange episode in Wild West history. There are hints of tension within the ranks, as Doc Holliday referred to in his interview in Denver. The group may have fragmented even before it got out of the Arizona Territory, with some of the lesser members heading their own way. The group had strayed far beyond legality by that point and perhaps some members feared that if it continued, the cowboys would put up a united front and start their own Vendetta Ride.

Thus the Vendetta Ride can be considered a failure. Wyatt Earp did not get the revenge he sought and he had to leave the town where he had established himself. The problem of crime along the border resolved itself through socioeconomic development rather than the blazing of six-shooters. Wyatt Earp and the other gunfighters of the Wild West had become throwbacks from an earlier time.

Tombstone's Boot Hill as it appears today. (David Lee Summers)

BIBLIOGRAPHY

Bowmaster, Patrick A., "A Fresh Look at 'Big Nose Kate,'" *Quarterly of the National Association for Outlaw and Lawmen History, Inc.*, July–September 1998

Boyer, Glenn G., "Morgan Earp: A Brother in the Shadow," *Old West,* Winter 1983

Breakenridge, William M., *Helldorado: Bringing the Law to the Mesquite*, University of Nebraska Press, Lincoln, NE (1992)

Burrows, Jack, *John Ringo: the Gunfighter Who Never Was,* University of Arizona Press, Tucson, AZ (1987)

Clum, John, "It All Happened in Tombstone," *Arizona Historical Quarterly*, October 1929

Cool, Paul, "It's Just A Flesh Wound: The Gunfights of Tombstone's Black Knight," Tombstone History Archives (www.tombstonehistoryarchives.com/?page_id=143, retrieved July 8, 2012)

Cunningham, Eugene, *Triggernometry: A Gallery of Gunfighters*, Corgi, London (1957)

Faulk, Odie B., *Tombstone: Myth and Reality,* Oxford University Press, New York, NY (1972)

Lake, Stuart N., *Wyatt Earp: Frontier Marshal*, Pocket, New York, NY (1994; first published 1931)

Marks, Paula Mitchell, *And Die in the West: The Story of the O.K. Corral Gunfight,* Morrow, New York, NY (1989)

Masterson, Bat, and Jack Demattos, *Famous Gunfighters of the Western Frontier,* R.M. Weatherford, Monroe, WA (1982; reprint of 1907 edition)

Palmquist, Robert F., "Mining Keno and the Law: The Tombstone Careers of Bob Winders, Charley Smith and Fred Dodge, 1879–1888," *The Journal of Arizona History*, Vol. 38, No. 2, Summer 1997

Roberts, Gary L., *Doc Holliday: The Life and Legend*, John Wiley and Sons, Inc., Hoboken, NJ (2007)

Shillingberg, William B., "Wyatt Earp and the Buntline Special Myth," *Kansas Historical Quarterly*, Vol. 42, No. 2, pages 113–54 (Summer 1976)

Shueh, Sam and Eric Chen, "Chinese Residents in Tombstone," *Tombstone Times* (www.tombstonetimes.com/stories/chinese.html, retrieved November 5, 2012)

Tanner, Karen Holliday, *Doc Holliday: A Family Portrait,* University of Oklahoma Press, Norman, OK (1998)

Terfertiller, Casey, *Wyatt Earp: The Life behind the Legend,* John Wiley and Sons, Inc., New York, NY (1997)

Turner, Alford E., ed., *The Earps Talk,* Creative Publishing Co., College Station, TX (1980)

Waters, Frank, *The Earp Brothers of Tombstone*, Bison Books, Lincoln, NE (1976)

INDEX

References to illustrations are shown in **bold**. References to plates are shown in **bold** with caption page in brackets, e.g. **70–71** (69).